The WELL HOUSE ·READER·

The
WELL HOUSE
·READER·

*Students Reflect on
Indiana University Bloomington
through the Years*

EDITED BY
DONALD GRAY

INDIANA UNIVERSITY PRESS

This book is a publication of
Indiana University Press
Office of Scholarly Publishing
Herman B Wells Library 350
1320 East 10th Street
Bloomington, Indiana 47405 USA
iupress.org

© 2022 by Donald J. Gray

All rights reserved
No part of this book may be reproduced or utilized in any form or by any means, electronic or mechanical, including photocopying and recording, or by any information storage and retrieval system, without permission in writing from the publisher. The paper used in this publication meets the minimum requirements of the American National Standard for Information Sciences—Permanence of Paper for Printed Library Materials, ANSI Z39.48-1992.

Manufactured in the United States of America

First printing 2022

Library of Congress Cataloging-in-Publication Data

Names: Gray, Donald J., editor.
Title: The Well House reader : students reflect on Indiana University Bloomington through the years / edited by Donald Gray.
Description: Bloomington, Indiana : Indiana University Press, 2022. | Series: Well House books
Identifiers: LCCN 2022024194 (print) | LCCN 2022024195 (ebook) | ISBN 9780253063908 (hardback) | ISBN 9780253063915 (paperback) | ISBN 9780253063922 (ebook)
Subjects: LCSH: Indiana University, Bloomington—Students—Attitudes. | Indiana University, Bloomington—History. | College students—Indiana—Bloomington—Attitudes.
Classification: LCC LD2521 .W45 2022 (print) | LCC LD2521 (ebook) | DDC 378.772/255—dc23/eng/20220713
LC record available at https://lccn.loc.gov/2022024194
LC ebook record available at https://lccn.loc.gov/2022024195

CONTENTS

Introduction   ix

PART ONE: THE CAMPUS AND THE TOWN

"To Kirkwood Hall," *Arbutus*, 1895   3

From *A Hoosier Holiday* (1916), Theodore Dreiser   4

"The Atmosphere of Indiana University," Two Overseas Men,
  The Hoosier, 1920   10

"It's in the Air," Ernie Pyle, *Indiana Daily Student*, 1922   14

From *The Stardust Road* (1946), Hoagy Carmichael   16

"Visions at Midnight," Ed Sovola, *Folio*, 1945   18

"The Mighty Jordan," Marlin Kinman, *Folio*, 1946   21

"Bloomington—A Sketch," Louise Foster, *Folio*, 1939   22

"Dundee of Bloomingshire," *The Date*, 1947   24

"Hiawatha, 1948," A. Nonymous, *The Crimson Bull*, 1948   26

"Rats, Waterbuckets, and Screaming," Bob Towns, *The Date*, 1946   28

"Yank on Bloomington Square," Hargis Westerfield, *Folio*, 1947   30

"Small Town Hippie Comics," art by R. T. Reece, *The Spectator*, 1969   31

"A Block Away from There: An Imitation of Frank O'Hara's
  A Step Away from There," Erin Chapman, *Canvas*, 2009   32

"Parking Lot at the Student Union," Steven Johnson, *Canvas*, 2016–17   34

"Frigid Venus," Gemma Lad, *Labyrinth*, 1992   35

PART TWO: STUDENTS

"Extracts from a Student's Diary, 1872," William T. Hicks, *Folio*, 1936   39

"The Simple but Touching Ballad of the Farmer Lad Who Changed,"
  The Hoosier, 1919   49

From *Initiation*, George Shively, 1925   50

"The End of the Very First Week," Roselda Zimmerman, *Folio*, 1937   54

"I Hate College Boys"; "I Love College Girls," *The Vagabond*, 1924   56

"The College Student: Juvenile Sophisticate," Nathan Davis, *The Vagabond*, 1924   60

"Woiking Goil," Elizabeth Flora Potts, *The Bored Walk*, 1931   64

"Won'erful Nell," Frank Smith, *The Vagabond*, 1925   66

Cover, *The Bored Walk*, art by Shannon M. Johnson, 1935   71

"Grasping Their Hard Earned and Long Sought after Sheepskins," *The Bored Walk*, 1933   72

"Taking Aim," Meredith Morgan, *Labyrinth*, 2005   74

"New Pens, Check," Adriana Valtierra, *Collins Columns*, 2012   76

"The Best Time of My Life," Mary-Katherine Lemon, *Collins Columns*, 2012   78

"Entirely Too Much Personal Information," Allison Neal, *Collins Columns*, 2019   79

Cover, *Books That Shaped Us*, art by Margaret Schnabel, *Collins Columns*, 2019   81

"Books, Babes, and Best Sellers," Margaret Schnabel, *Collins Columns*, 2019   82

PART THREE: FACULTY

"Departments," art by George Brehm, *Arbutus* 1903   87

"Indiana," by Don Herold, *College Humor*, 1929   88

Cover, "But Ted, I Didn't Know," art by Normabelle Heiman, *The Bored Walk*, 1940   93

"Carl Eigenmann," art in *Arbutus*, 1899   94

"A Skinner Box Named Meyer," Warren Blumenfeld, *The Crimson Bull*, 1954   95

"Textbooks Unbound," Mike Schwimmer, *The Crimson Bull*, 1954   99

"The Physics-cal Side of Love," Myrtle V. Schneller, *Folio*, 1944   103

"A Geometry Test," Sieglinde Lim, *Calliope*, 1994   106

"Precipice," John W. Stein, *Folio*, 1939   107

"25 Reasons Why You Should Attend Summer Sessions," ad in
   The Crimson Bull, 1949   108

"This Is What I Do in Class," art by Emily Francisco,
   Collins Columns, 2012   109

PART FOUR: ROMANCE

"For Man Is a Giddy Thing," Grace Smith, *Arbutus*, 1903   113

"At the Well House," Gilbert Swaim, *The Bored Walk*, 1932   119

"So Then I Said," art by Doan Helms Jr., *The Crimson Bull*, 1948   125

"Instant Idyll on the Third Floor of Ballantine Hall 2:24 P.M.,"
   Garry Emmons, *Quarry*, 1972   126

"Just Friends," Tim Dohrer, *Labyrinth*, 1990   128

"Bloomington Lawyer: Stay," Betsy Tandy, *Quarry*, 1974   130

"One Night Stand," Collinda Taylor, *Labyrinth*, 2007   131

"Yes, These People Exist," Emily Francisco, *Collins Columns*, 2012   132

PART FIVE: PROTESTS

"Our President's Origin," *The Dagger*, 1875   137

"The Ku Klux Klan Has Been on the Kampus, Is on the Kampus, and
   Will Be on the Kampus," *The Vagabond*, 1924   138

"Dirge for the Khaki Youth," Bob Meyer, *The Bored Walk*, 1940   141

"No!" Richard Reed, *Folio*, 1939   142

"Education or Mass Production?" Albert C. Losche, *Folio*, 1942   144

"Tolerance: Will It Be Future Perfect?" Jayne Walpole,
   The Date, 1946   147

"Concerto," Bernice Cohen, *Folio*, 1944   149

From *The Translator*, John Crowley, 2002   151

"OH No! CRUD Strikes Again," George Metsky, *The Spectator*, 1970   158

Cover, *The Spectator*, art by R. T. Reese, 1970   161

"Voice," Jim Carr, *Quarry* 1973   162

"The 60s in the 80s—Almost," Dave Bender, *Arbutus*, 1987   163

PART SIX: DEPARTURES

"Sea of Life," art by Don Herold, *Arbutus*, 1911   167

"On Entering the Campus," *Arbutus*, 1915   168

"There's Another Side of College with a Different Education," Robert Smith, *Arbutus*, 1983   169

"The Bird," John Schuster, *Labyrinth*, 2000   176

Appendix: Student Publications at Indiana University Bloomington   185

Notes   195

Acknowledgments   199

INTRODUCTION

This anthology is founded in my reading of reminiscences about Indiana University Bloomington in books and essays by Theodore Dreiser, Hoagy Carmichael, and Don Herold, in novels by university graduates George Shively and John Crowley, and in campus magazines whose editors and contributors were students in residence at the time of publication. I began by looking for descriptions of the physical campus: poems like the one celebrating the construction of Kirkwood Hall in the campus yearbook, *Arbutus*, in 1895, and the narrative of a walk down the banks of the Jordan River and out onto Kirkwood Avenue in the student magazine *Canvas* in 2009. But I soon realized that I was reading not just about the landscape and buildings of the campus but also about the student life conducted in its precincts. When Hoagy Carmichael describes the low stone wall on the south border of the campus in the 1920s, for example, he populates it with "spooning" couples, and in his account of the campus hangout the Book Nook, the room jumps with the pulse of students talking, listening to or playing music, dancing, even writing poetry. What started, then, as a kind of literary adjunct to J. Terry Clapacs's splendid history and display of the grounds and architecture of the campus (*Indiana University Bloomington: America's Legacy Campus*: Bloomington, 2017) became an assembly of writing and art about students at work and, more often, at play during their years on the campus, their pleasures and commitments, their anxieties and anger, and their ideas about the worth and possibilities of their education.

As material for a social history of campus life in Bloomington, this collection is of course partial, inflected by the interests and convictions of those who wrote memoirs and fiction about their time on campus and of the students who wrote and drew for the thirty or so campus magazines I have read. Most nineteenth-century students did not attend the meetings of the campus's literary societies, which often included talks on or readings from literature. Many did not go to the Book Nook in the 1920s to hear Hoagy Carmichael play the piano. Most students probably did not care much about the gossip in the campus magazines of the 1930s and 1940s about who got pinned or engaged. Many students did not go out to the country to swim in the quarries ("There's Another Side of College"). Nor did most students join in the protest march down Seventh Avenue reconstructed in John Crowley's novel *The Translator*, or join in the attacks on the marchers. In the novel, when two students are asked if they represent one of the campus peace groups organizing the march, one replies, "We are it."

Hundreds of thousands of students went to classes and labs, wrote their papers and took their exams, and made their grades and graduated during the past century and a half. But there is not much about learning in the campus magazines I have read. When these writers or artists entered a classroom, it was almost always to depict or describe students falling asleep, coming late, cheating, or importuning an instructor for a better grade. In a cartoon in *The Bored Walk*, a professor—moustache, bow tie, monocle, a cut perhaps borrowed from a different joke—asks a young woman, "You missed my class this morning, didn't you?" "No, not at all, Professor," she replies (February 1932, 25.) It is perhaps to the same point that although for decades the yearbook *Arbutus* has given dozens of pages each year to athletics, I found a lot of sport news but only one short story in these campus magazines about an athletic event—a baseball game (*Arbutus*, 1899)—and one fable about the Little 500 (*Crimson Bull*, 1956).

Instead, in their art and writing about the campus, students have used what they saw in magazines and movies and learned in their reading and classes to describe their experience in college and to wonder about what would come next. In poetry and fiction, they have explored the chances of becoming someone new on this new ground—not just meeting new people and trying out new adventures but, as the hero of George Shively's novel *Initiation* puts it at the start of his time at the university, the possibility of "thinking yourself through." They made up poems and short stories to look at the pleasures and disappointments of romance. They employed the conventions of fantasy and satire to go up against the Ku Klux Klan, the university administration, and what they saw as the errors of their government. They used lyrics to celebrate the solution of a mathematical problem and the missed chance of romance and to capture the wonder that they got here at all ("the game requires so much skill/it might as well be chance"). Even in writing that was as much editorial as imaginative, they adopted the tactics and cadences of artful polemicists like H. L. Mencken and William Buckley. In 1925, a writer in *Arbutus*—the style and sentiment suggest it was Philip Blair Rice, one of the founders of the undergraduate magazine *The Vagabond* and a member of the yearbook staff—argued that the purpose of a public university is not to educate "a few geniuses . . . but to enable the greatest possible number of people to live, work, and play just a little more understandingly, a little more vividly than they would otherwise" (31). Those are the gifts of a literary and esthetic as well as a liberal education, and the students represented in this collection, and many others, used art and writing to do what art and literature can always do: help them make sense of where they were and what was happening to them and try out who they could become.

The
WELL HOUSE
·READER·

PART ONE
·The Campus and the Town·

To Kirkwood Hall

Kirkwood! Thou art not merely stone and sand;
But human spirit, energy and art
In thee are manifest. Each visible part
Reveals the impress of a master hand;
Thou are unto our educated land
A generating work of Truth. The heart
Of Wisdom shall, in feeling throbs, impart
To thee, Truth's childhood bed, divinely planned,
While coursing subtlest life through thy veins,
Muscular, sand-walled, cold and dead—
A glowing, living, spiritual influence,
Thy walls shall burst in body-rending pain,
As Zeus' head, to free thy offspring bred
To grow to higher things, life more immense.

From *Arbutus*, 1895, 35.

From *A Hoosier Holiday* (1916)

BY THEODORE DREISER

Theodore Dreiser (1871–1945) dropped out of high school in Warsaw, Indiana, and moved to Chicago, where he worked in a series of menial jobs. One of his high school teachers found him there, persuaded him to enroll in Indiana University, and helped him financially. His year in Bloomington—1889–90—was unsettled and mostly unhappy, and he left to work his way east in a series of newspaper jobs until he landed in New York. There, he eventually became the editor of several women's magazines and wrote his first novel, Sister Carrie (1900), which was reluctantly put out by a publisher who objected to the sexual immorality of its heroine and to the plot, in which the characters' fates are powerfully affected by natural and social forces beyond their control. Dreiser went on to become an important and esteemed novelist in this mode of literary naturalism, most notably in An American Tragedy *(1925).*

In A Hoosier Holiday, *Dreiser, a driver, and a friend, who is an illustrator, travel by automobile westward along the route he followed on his journey to New York. When he gets to Bloomington, he describes the campus and town both as they were when he lived and studied there and as they appear a quarter of a century later.*

In approaching this town my mind was busy with another group of reminiscences. As I thought back over them now, it seemed to me that I must have been a most unsatisfactory youth to contemplate at this time, one who lacked nearly all of the firm, self-directive qualities which most youths of my age at that time were supposed to have.

I was eighteen then, and all romance and moon-shine. I had come down from Chicago after these several years at Warsaw and two in Chicago, in which I had been trying to connect commercially with life, and as I may say now, I feel myself to have been a rather poor specimen. I had no money other than about three hundred dollars loaned to me, or rather forced upon me, by an ex-teacher of mine (one who had conducted the recitation room in the high school at Warsaw) who, finding me working for a large wholesale hardware company in Chicago, insisted that I should leave and come here to be educated.

"You may never learn anything directly there, Theodore" she counseled, "but something will come to you indirectly. You will see what education means, what its aim is and that will be worth a great deal. Just go one year, at least, then you can decide for yourself what you want to do after that." (pp. 482–83) . . .

I know now for a fact that I never learned, all the time I was there, quite what it was all about. I heard much talk of -ologies and -tries and -isms without quite grasping the fundamental fact that they were really dealing with plain, ordinary, everyday life—the forces about us. Somehow I had the vague uncertain notion that they did not concern ordinary life at all. I remember one brisk youth telling me that in addition to law, which he was studying, he was taking up politics, taxation, economics, and the like, as aids. I wondered of what possible use those things could be to him, and how much superior his mind must be to mine, since he could grasp them and I, no doubt, could not.

Again, the professors there were such a wondrous company to me, quite marvelous. They were such an outré company, your heavy-domed, owl-like wiseacres, who see in books and the storing up of human knowledge in books the sum and substance of life's significance. As I look back on them now I marvel at my awe of them then, and at that time I was not very much awestricken either—rather nonplussed.

Suffice it to say that the one thing that I really wanted [now] to see in connection with this college was a ground floor parlor I had occupied in an old, rusty, vine-covered house, which stood in the center of a pleasing village lawn and had for a neighbor a small, one-story frame, where dwelt a hoyden of a girl who made it her business to bait me the first semester I was there. This room I had occupied with a law student by the name of William or Bill Wadhams, center rush and almost guiding spirit of the whole college football team, and afterwards county treasurer of and state senator from an adjacent Indiana county. He was a romping, stamping, vigorous, black-haired, white-faced pagan, who cursed and drank a little and played cards and flirted with the girls. He could be so mild and so engaging that when I first saw him I liked him immensely, and what was much more curious he seemed to take a fancy to me.

We made an agreement as to expenditures and occupying the same room. It did not seem in the least odd to me, at that time, that he should occupy the same bed with me. I had always been sleeping with one or the other of my brothers. It was more odd that, although he at once surrounded himself with the creme-de-la-crème of the college football world, who made of our humble chamber a conference and card room, I got along well enough with them all to endure it, and even made friends out of some of them. They were charming—so robust and boisterous and contentious and yet genial.... BLOOMINGTON, as we sped into it, did not seem much changed from the last time I had laid eyes upon it, twenty-five years before, only now, having seen the more picturesque country to the south of it, I did not think the region in which it lay seemed as broken and diversified as it did the year I first came to it.... Now it seemed more or less tame, and in addition it had grown so in size and architectural pretentiousness, as to have obliterated most of that rural inadequacy and backwoods charm which had been its most delightful characteristic to me in 1889.

Then it was so poor and so very simple. The court house square had been a gem of moss-back simplicity and poverty, more attractive even, rurally speaking, than that court house I just mentioned as being the charm of Paoli. Here, also, the hitching rail had extended all around the square. I saw more tumble-down wagons, rheumatic and broken-down men, old, brown, almost moss covered coats and thin, bony, spavined horses in the Bloomington of 1889 than I ever saw anywhere before or since. In addition to this, in spite of the smallness of the college, many of the six hundred students had considerable money, for Indiana was a prosperous state and these youths and girls were very well provided for. Secret or Greek letter societies and college social circles of different degrees of import abounded. There were college rakes and college loafers and college swells. At that time the university chanced to have a faculty which, because of force and brains, was attracting considerable attention. David Starr Jordan, afterwards President of Leland Stanford, was president here. [Joseph] Swain, afterwards President of Swarthmore, was professor of mathematics. Rufus L. Green, a man who made considerable stir in mathematics and astronomy in later years, was associate in the chair of mathematics. Jeremiah Jenks, a man who figured conspicuously in American sociological and political discussion in after life and added considerable luster to the fame of Cornell, was occupying the chair of sociology and political economy. Edward Howard Griggs, a man who has carried culture, with a large C, into all the women's clubs and intellectual movements of one kind and another from ocean to ocean, was occupying an assistant professorship in literature. There was [Herman] Von Holst, called to the chair of history at the University of Chicago, and so on—a quite interesting and scintillating galaxy of educative minds.

The student body, of which I was such an unsatisfactory unit, seemed quite well aware of the character and import of the men above them, educationally. There was constant and great talk concerning the relative merits of each and every one. As Miss Fielding, my sponsor and mentor, had predicted, I learned more concerning the seeming import of education, the branches of knowledge and the avenues and vocations open to men and women in the intellectual world, than I had ever dreamed existed—and just from hearing the students argue, apotheosize, anathematize, or apostrophize one course or one professor or another. Here I met my first true radicals—young men who disagreed vigorously and at every point with the social scheme and dogma as they found it. Here I found the smug conventionalists and grinds seeking only to carve out the details of a profession and subsequently make a living. Here I found the flirt, the college widow, and the youth with purely socializing tendencies, who found in college life a means of gratifying an intense and almost chronic desire for dancing, dressing, spooning, living in a world of social airs and dreams.

There were, oddly enough, hard and chronic religionists even among the incoming class, who were bent upon preaching "the kingdom of God is at hand" to all the world. They seemed a little late to me, even at that day and date, though I was still not quite sure myself....

Entering Bloomington this afternoon, the memories of all my old aches and pains were exceedingly dim. We say to ourselves at many particular times, "I will never forget this," or, "The pain of this will endure forever," but, alas, even our most treasured pains and sufferings escape us. We are compelled to admit that the memory of that which rankled so is very dim. Marsh fires, all of us. We are made to glow by the heat and radiance of certain days, but we fade—and we vanish.

Nevertheless, entering Bloomington now it had some charm, only as I thought the whole thing over the memory of my various sex failures still rankled. "I was not really happy here," I told myself. "I was in too transient and inadequate a mood." And perhaps that was true. At any rate, I wanted to see this one principal room I have previously mentioned, and the college and the court house, and feel the general atmosphere of the place.

As a whole, the town was greatly changed, but not enough to make it utterly different. One could still see the old town in the new. For although the old, ramshackle, picturesque attractive court house had been substituted by a much larger and more imposing building of red brick and white stone—a not uninteresting design—still a number of the buildings which had formerly surrounded it were here. The former small and by no means cleanly post office, with its dingy paper and knife marked writing shelf on one side, had been replaced by a handsome government building suitable for a town of thirty or forty thousand. A new city hall, a thing unthought of in my day, was being erected in a street just south of the square. New bank buildings, dry goods stores, drug store, restaurants, were all in evidence. In my time there had been but two restaurants, both small, and one almost impossible. Now there were four or five quite respectable ones, and one of considerable pretensions. In addition, down the Main Street could be seen the college, or university, a striking group of buildings entirely different from those I had known. A picture postcard, referring to one of the buildings, spoke of five thousand population for the city, and a four thousand attendance for the University. (pp. 496–97) . . .

After this came the university, wholly changed, but far more attractive than it had been in my day—a really beautiful school. I could find only a few things—Wylie Hall, the brook, a portion of some building which had formerly been our library. It had been so added to that it was scarcely recognizable. I ran back in memory to all those whom I had known here—the young men, the women, the professors. Where were they all? Suddenly I felt dreadfully lonely, as though I had been shipwrecked on a desert island. Not a soul did I know any more of all those who had been here; scarcely one could I definitely place. What is life that it can thus obliterate itself, I asked myself. If a whole realm of interests and emotions can thus definitely pass, what is anything?

From *A Hoosier Holiday* (London and New York: John Lane, 1916), 484–90, 496–97, 503.

The Atmosphere of Indiana University

BY TWO OVERSEAS MEN

IN ADDITION TO prohibition, profiteering and strikes, the war has given us many things. It is true that our morals and institutions were not revolutionized as many people hoped they might be, but the war did give to hundreds of thousands of young men a new outlook on life, a broader and a deeper comprehension of the true value of living.

To many, a college education has ceased to be superficial but has become a vital and important means of securing a true appreciation of the forces and motives that go to make up the fabric of our national existence. Moved by the ever-present danger in the lurking shadow of death, by the sight of comrades and friends killed and strong men maimed and mutilated beyond recognition, thousands of men have returned from France determined to secure the most from life. Many of them came back to their universities and colleges filled with eagerness and a hope that the changes wrought in themselves might be echoed and reflected in changes in university life. What have they found?

Of conditions at other schools and colleges we are not competent to judge, but we do feel that there is something wrong at Indiana University. Returned soldiers and sailors are not generally Bolshevists and I. W. W.'s [International Workers of the World]; they are not "reds" or radicals, but level-headed, matter-of-fact Americans who have broadened the horizon of their experience, until they now have the point of view of citizens of the world as well as citizens of Indiana. We are not in sympathy with all new reforms, but we are heartily in favor of altering some conditions at Indiana University.

The social atmosphere at Indiana is largely at fault for most of these unsatisfactory conditions. Many of us come from homes in which the general atmosphere is so superior to the atmosphere at Indiana that we find the change not only devoid of inspiration, but actually a shock at first and later a dulling narcotic influence which saps originality and freezes inspiration. Here we find conversation keyed to the low level of the intellectually atrophied instead of raised to the level of those who have fresher outlooks and broader points of view.

At home we are accustomed to some discussion of subjects of national and international interest. Politics, religion and literature are not wholly ignored in conversations about the dinner table or in gatherings of friends. Here we find an anaemic dribble about clothes and appearances, a wearying stream of comment on the last or the next dance. But even this chatter is perhaps better than the "smut sessions" which occupy the valuable time of many undergraduates.

The guiding motive in the life of many campus organizations seems to be "policy." Some organizations go so far as to dictate to their members whom they shall associate with in order to keep up the social standing of the organization.

People who make any sort of pretense of originality are immediately dubbed "nuts," and are silenced by choruses of groans, while the intellectually honest are entirely without the pale of the ordinary student's comprehension. In our center of culture, the Book Nook, which is the intellectual yard stick of the University and where books are of no importance and nooks of supreme importance, do we find enlightening conversation, spontaneity, originality, new movements discussed? No. We find "scolleging," and the supreme scollegers are those who can "get by without cracking a book." [On the Book Nook, see note on p. 17]

It is necessary that we have our pleasure. Psychology teaches us that we must have diversions, outlets for superfluous energies; but students can find more beneficial recreation than "mugging," "candying," and "scolleging." Hours spent in strolling the paths of the campus may be well spent if the University is to serve as a matrimonial bureau for the State, and parents who send their sons and daughters here for that purpose are usually amply recompensed for their sacrifice.

Perhaps there is a place in the University for "candy-asses" [see description of "candies" in "I Hate College Boys," p. 56] but when their importance becomes such that they mould college life and control the atmosphere, then the more serious students have to look outside the University for inspiration and enlightenment. Under present conditions we cannot expect the limelight now thrown upon athletics and movie stars to be shared by scientists, authors, philosophers and artists.

Fundamentally provincialism and local-mindedness lie behind the atmosphere of our University life and are largely responsible for its nature. We are all Hoosiers, and are naturally proud of it, as we most certainly have a right to be, but we continue to pat ourselves on the back and revolve in the same narrow and restricted orbit with our eyes toward the center. Our idolizing of James Whitcomb Riley and our loyalty to him serve to illustrate this attitude of mind admirably. To an unbiased critic his honeyed sentimentality and jingling, jiggy rhythm would not give him a place among the great poets. His poetry corresponds to the best poetry as ragtime corresponds to music. Many of us enjoy ragtime and most of us enjoy Riley in limited doses, but in Indiana Riley is canonized and his work placed above criticism.

This provincialism is not entirely confined to the student body. It seeps down from high places permeating the whole structure and fabric of the University, suppressing and stifling freshness and freedom of action.

For example, the University boasts a newspaper which it sees fit to dignify with the name of "The Indiana Daily Student." This paper never employs destructive criticism in its columns but tries always to be optimistic and complimentary by boosting everything. The following incident is a conservative example: Some months ago a member of the Mantell Company lectured to a large body of students and recited as masterpieces of English literature some examples of the most sentimental atrocities which our literature possesses. One of them was "Aux Italiens" [by the nineteenth-century British writer Edward Bulwer-Lytton], pronounced by the reader to be one of the supreme peaks in the mountain ranges of literature. An indignant auditor resented this estimate and wrote a satire for "The Student" concerning the incident, with the result that the satire was suppressed. No matter how conscientious and sincere the student members of its editorial staff may be, no matter how honest and straight-forward their expressions of opinions, any criticism of the University is either censored before publication, or the editors are severely reprimanded and chastised. Such procedure has resulted in a soulless "Student," wholly unrepresentative of student thought or student opinion. It has become nothing more or less than a glorified bulletin board.

We had hoped this centennial year that long strides might be made, that the University might at last strike out boldly, herald its past and provide for the future. But it seems that we must be cautious, avoid treading on toes, and bow to precedents.

The material welfare of the University will be taken care of in the future if we can place reliance in our state legislature. Governor [James P.] Goodrich stated in a speech this year that "we have not done as much for higher education in Indiana as we should have done, nor as much as we will do in the immediate future."

But if we wish to change or improve the social atmosphere about us we must first start with ourselves. There must be more investigation, more reading, an interest in world problems and world movements, more originality, more criticism and idol-smashing scepticism. When such a state of mind has been attained then the various activities and enterprises about the University will be imbued with a new life and a new energy, and we can move and speak and live freely, unhampered by the thought of censor or un-restrained by respect for policy.

From *The Hoosier* II, April 1920, 30–35.

"It's in the Air"

BY ERNIE PYLE

Ernie Pyle (1900–45) grew up on a farm near Dana, Indiana. After he graduated from high school, he enlisted in the Naval Reserve—the United States had entered World War I in Europe, but it ended before he completed his training. In 1919, he enrolled as a student on the Bloomington campus. He wrote for Arbutus and the Daily Student, and after his junior year he served as editor of the summer edition of the Student. In 1923, a semester short of graduation, he left school to work as a reporter at an Indiana newspaper and soon moved on to a newspaper job in Washington, DC. In the 1930s, he began traveling around the country and writing a series of very popular columns about the places he saw and the ordinary people he met. When the United States entered World War II, he went first to Europe and then to the Pacific as a journalist, writing the same kind of human interest stories about the soldiers and sailors fighting the war. He was killed by enemy fire in April 1945 during the invasion of Okinawa.

Nearly everyone who has ever attended Indiana University will tell you there is no place in the world like Indiana. They sometimes attempt to explain that statement but they cannot.

Strangely enough in their attempt to explain, they fail to mention the assets of the school usually mentioned by its boosters. They have nothing to say about the remarkable professors whose fame seems so much greater in the outside world than it does to the students who work under them. They do not mention the buildings or equipment or the many advantages carefully compiled in the school catalog. They do not gather together and present facts which a logical speaker would use in convincing folk that this is a great school.

Ex-students recognize the value of all these things, recognize their argumentative value. But when they ejaculate that there is no place in all the world like Indiana, they are thinking about something else. They are thinking of spring days when the campus is bursting with fragrance, vivid with the color of blossoms and new leaves, and when the moon is bright—it is undeniable that spring is nowhere in the world as it is at Indiana. They are thinking about the autumn evenings when dusk has settled and the last cheers have died out over Jordan Field [now the Union parking lot], and another football game has become a memory, another football game which may or may not have been a victory but which was a courageous fight by Indiana men whom everyone in school knew and liked. They are thinking of "pep" meetings and mass meetings and pow-wows in which Indiana men sounded the ancient battle cry, where sheepish football captains tried to make speeches before a howling crowd of students and equally wild old grads, and where the old songs gave at the same time a sudden impulse to tears and an electric thrill down the backbone. They are thinking about hundreds of wholesome, pleasant people, who were their friends. They are thinking something about Indiana which none of them could ever express in words.

These persons who make such broad unqualified statements about Indiana say that they have since tried out living in many other places but that somehow the tang is missing. Other schools can contain nothing after such moments. Other schools seem to lack the facilities to produce those thrills which certainly can come within but four years of a lifetime.

These are the feelings of those who have been here and have left. Perhaps it is foolish and sentimental but they will affirm it is the truth.

From *Indiana Daily Student*, September 5, 1922, 4.

From *The Stardust Road* (1946)

BY HOAGY CARMICHAEL

Born in Bloomington, Hoagland Carmichael attended the local high school and went on to receive a bachelor's degree from Indiana University in 1925 and a law degree in 1926. All during his college years, he played piano at dances and in campus hangouts like the Book Nook and organized his own bands and booked other bands, including some that included Bix Beiderbecke, for fraternity dances. He briefly practiced law in Florida, but after his first songs were published he moved to New York and eventually to Hollywood, where he wrote songs for movies in which he sometimes also sang and performed.

The Book Nook, frequently mentioned in memoirs and short stories, was on Indiana Avenue opposite the site now occupied by Bryan Hall.

Have you ever seen the big maples? The trunks are sometimes three feet in diameter and they shoot straight up, barren of branches, for some forty or fifty feet and then they spread out into a huge umbrella of limbs and foliage. Hundreds of these and an equal number of large beech trees shade the Indiana campus. For many years there were no walks—just natural paths winding among the trees. Several of these led to a street that borders the campus on the east [Jordan Avenue[1]], called Sorority Row, and here is where the quartets and the jazz bands serenaded at night.

A low stone wall borders the campus on the south. This is the "spooning wall" and is usually dotted by quiet indiscernible couples late at night who have stopped there on the way home from the Book Nook or a picture show. To the north of the campus, bounding Dunn Meadows and the old athletic fields, runs the famous Jordan River. Famous because of its high-sounding name and yet its waters—a foot deep in floodtime—barely trickle during the dog days of August. But never let it be said that this jaded stream produced nothing. It did. Crustaceans. Crawdads I mean, by the thousands. We kids were not barefoot boys with rod and reel, we were barefoot boys with tin can for scooping them up. Fishing for crawdads is an art. It's like catching a fly with your hand and almost as difficult. Indiana Avenue is the other boundary and thereon stands the Book Nook.

The Book Nook was a little house originally. It was situated hard by the campus on Indiana Avenue and it really was a book store. Gradually it had grown and been added to until it seated a hundred or so Coke-guzzling, book-laden, high-spirited students. There new tunes were heard and praised; lengthy discussions were started and never quite finished. There the first steps of the toddle were taken and fitted to our new rhythm. Dates were made and hopes were born. Jordan's band [Howard Jordan's orchestra, out of Louisville] continued playing for the local dances and sometimes they could be prevailed upon to stay over and play for a Sunday afternoon session in the Book Nook. *"Shake it and break it, and hang it on the wall"*—that was the Sunday ritual.

Let me take you gently by the hand and lead you into the Book Nook on a normal afternoon. That little guy, over there, flogging the piano—that could be me. The one with the long nose and the exerted purple face. And the large freckled youth with the saxophone, the one making those long blue notes, that's Batty De Marcus. The high-cheekboned unshaved youth perched yonder in a booth, that's Moenkhaus,[2] composing a poem, perhaps, for we hear his weird coyote-howl laugh even above our efforts.

A few couples are seated in booths at the far side and Pete Costas, the proprietor, is punctuating his English with Greek epithets because Klondike Tucker, the Negro chef, has balled up an order....

Those round yellow objects arising as the twilight creeps softly upon the scene? Why, those are grapefruit rinds hurled at me because my music has grown too sedate.

I dodge the grapefruit rinds and stop. Monk is going to read his creation. There is a moment of quiet. Quiet fraught with expectancy. Nerves too tight. Minds keyed to vistas beyond the horizons of so-called rational thought.

From *The Stardust Road* (New York: Rinehart, 1946), 33–35.

Visions at Midnight

BY ED SOVOLA

I WALKED ALONE at midnight through the campus and of these things I did think. I was in front of the library when both hands of the clock on the Student Building pointed toward the stars. Twelve o'clock! The seconds that remained before the clock was to chime the beginning of another day seemed interminably long. I stood in confused anticipation of the first chime. Then ... the knell of a new day began.

I moved on thinking of the boys and girls who were starting at Indiana University. I wondered how many at this moment were lying awake in their beds ... thinking ... thinking ... of their new friends, of their studies, of Mom and Dad, of the letter they had written earlier in the evening, which didn't tell the whole story because they were so mixed up at everything.... Thinking ... thinking ... of tomorrow.

I looked back at the heavily shadowed library and remembered the inscription above the door. I couldn't see it but I read it ... word for word. "A Good Book is the Precious Lifeblood of a Master Spirit" [Milton]. A truth I wished l hadn't abused so many times. A truth I hoped many new boys and girls would notice above the library entrance and remember as they pursued education.

I walked towards Maxwell Hall. I wished I had at my side some boy who was enrolled in pre-law. I would show him his goal, law school, at its prettiest. [Until the 1950s, Maxwell Hall housed the School of Law.] The night, casting a gossamer mantle of black over the building, fusing it with the sky, enhanced immeasurably its beauty to the aesthetic eye or to an excited youth, so vulnerable to impressionism.

After the splendor of the night and the enthusiasm of youthful hope and dream did their work I would try to vaccinate this boy against the pitfalls he would experience before he could enter the school he had chosen and which he now so proudly associates himself with by saying, "I'm a pre-law."

"Keep that goal ever before your eyes," I would say to him, "for you yourself are master or slave of the events that will decide your fate."

I looked to my left and saw the Union Building. A jewel that rose high against a background of twinkling stars. I thought of the Commons, where there is so much opportunity for good fellowship. A place where the lighter side of college life often has its beginning for the new student. A place where he might be introduced to a girl who in a short while will be his "steady." A place where a group of people that seemed so likeable yet were so remote to him suddenly and happily made him a part of themselves.

I turned to the "Main-Drag" of the campus. Wylie Hall, Kirkwood, Science [Lindley] Hall, stood silent and foreboding, for their Spirit had left them. That spirit was in the students. But that life, I knew, would flow in with the morning, and no longer would they be empty shells.

Looking into the wooded area opposite these buildings I thought how much the campus could be likened unto a woman. I have often thought of this juxtaposition after I realized I was in love with my campus. I thought how much more meaning there was to my life after this realization. I wished every new student would have that experience. It means so very much to their happiness and to their welfare.

I make my comparison of the campus to a woman from personal experience. Now, I thought, they see the campus in its full beauty, painted in the bright colors of Fall. But, they will also see the campus, bleak, cold, shorn of all adornment in the throes of winter. They will walk in exhilaration of little accomplishments in studies and in their social life; they will walk in a saddened and fretful state after they experience unexpected setbacks. They will know days of humdrum, unexciting existence. They will have conflicts with their nature, their personality, as they move from day to day among the identities called students and professors. They will have to accept responsibilities. They will thrill to the excitement of completion and progress as one semester draws to a close. They will see their mistakes, their successes.

The first warm breath of coming Spring will be another beginning for them. They will see the metamorphosis of returning beauty. Just as mysterious and imperceptible as the returning leaves and flowers will be their growth in mind and spirit. They will have seen in one cycle, the good, the bad, the exciting.

As it is with someone loved, when they leave for a short while, they will have the curious feeling that they miss something or someone. There will be a vacuum in their persons that can be filled, during that era called their college career, only by going back from whence they came. They will be in love, and it will be pleasant.

I made my way through the campus at midnight, and I thought of these things and the boys and girls who were beginning a new life here at I.U.

From *Folio* XI:1 (1945), 305–307.

The Mighty Jordan

BY MARLIN KINMAN

Mightily the Jordan flows
Between the hills of Bloomington,
Mighty with its sweeping bends,
Treacherous currents and waterfalls,
Thunders down across the campus
At whose bend brave children wade;
Fearful they tremble at their daring.
Rises now the mighty Jordan
With the fall of every rain,
Rising from its banks of grass,
Spreading terror as it rises,
Sweeping over fertile plains.
Yet, only in I.U.'s old legends
Is the Jordan e'en a river.

Note: Apologies to Mr. Longfellow ["The Song of Hiawatha"]

From *Folio* XI:4 (1946), 47.

Bloomington

A Sketch

BY LOUISE FOSTER

4:30—One end of town trudges to work
Disliking everything about their jobs,
Still hoping that someday they will get a break and can go to Detroit
Where the real money is.

7:00—The drowsy city resumes life, children fuss, mothers scold,
High-schoolers snooze a while longer, then grab books; and rush schoolward.
They are longing for the time when they'll be grown-up
And can find the real money.

8:00—The campus becomes alive with the rush, swish, of students.
Day after day we collegians stick it out, hoping . . . dreaming
Of the day we'll be up in the world
Where the real money is.

12:00—The town, tired at the half of the day,
Curses the unjustices of the world.
As if by mutual agreement it strives to find something stronger
To bring in the real money.

7:00—Casting off their cloaks of the workaday world
All forget themselves in small-town pleasure with the thought, if any, of—
"What's the use anyway? Have a good time while you can!"
They'll never find the real money.

Bloomington—a transient
Where no one is really satisfied.
It is fired with the ambition to move on
Where the real money is.

From *Folio* IV:3 (1939), 6.

Dundee of Bloomingshire

DR. HAMILTON SMITH-CARRUTHERS WEMBLY, of Oxford University, revealed in a recent monograph his amazing discovery of a short scene from the fifth act of Shakespeare's *Henry V*. He told of examining an ancient quarto and finding the lines below, omitted in all other known versions. (Authentication will be supplied on request by the editors.)

SCENE III. ENGLAND. A STREET OF BLOOMINGSHIRE.
Enter FIRTH and DUNDEE, soldiers of England.

FIR. Then ho, my noble comrade! Now the wars
Are fought, is it that thou would woo
The muse of knowledge and would fain pursue
The banner of learned men who fill
The pates of blockheads such as we who are
Returned to peaceful life from Agincourt?

DUN. It doth behoove me to avail myself
Of aught that can be turned to use in life.
But I am come from newly fallen hopes;
For all who dwell in Bloomingshire hath told
Me lodgings are as scarce as virtues of
The Fiend himself. And so I now depart
And soon will hie me back to hall and hearth.
But since I have this dream to conquer all
That men can learn, I'll never yield it up.

Perchance these rendered plans of mine will once
Again unite, and I'll attain my goal.

FIR. A pox upon the housing office, whence
Comes naught but grief; a sorry state indeed.

DUN. Oh woe! Woe!

FIR. By all that's sacred, noble Dundee! Hold
From tearing garb and clenching teeth in vain.
Come, join me at the friendly hostelry
Of Nikolas of Greece, where one can drop
One's pains into a flagon brimming o'er,
And quaff them down with mighty draughts to soothe.

DUN. Aye, thou hast spoken well; and let us to
The Greek's betake us—Bloomingshire will scorn
Me; but I'll wager Bacchus will receive. (Exeunt.)

From *The Date*, October 1947, 14.

Hiawatha, 1948

BY A. NONYMOUS

Down along the Tenth Street speedway,
Where it intersects with Woodlawn,
Stood the trailer of a vet'ran,
Trailer of a student veteran.
Dark behind it stood the Fieldhouse,
To the east the football stadium
With its cheering fans assembled.
In his little Indian Trailer
Lived he with his wife and children.
Slept, and cooked, and ate, and studied,
Carried to and fro his buckets,
Washed his clothing in the Bendix.

There his little wife resided,
Nursed the little Hiawatha,
Tucked him in his folding carriage,
Stilled his fretful wails by saying,
"Hush! Your pappy's cracking textbooks!"

Many things his mama taught him
Of the rods and pods on campus,
Showed him "joes" down in the Commons,
Showed him "Papa's Comp professor,"
Begged him not to kick his shinbones.

And he learned the campus's language,
Learned he of a mid-term "smoke-up,"[3]

Observed he well the art of "cramming,"
Learned to dread the thought of finals,
When he watched his papa, red-eyed,
Drinking java 'til the wee hours.
Learned to say unto his father,
"JEEPERS! POP, I HOPE YOU PASS!"

From *The Crimson Bull*, March 1948, 9.

Rats, Waterbuckets, and Screaming

BY BOB TOWNS

KIDS ARE THE main courses of study over at Woodlawn Court; and most former G.I.'s claim that World War II was a snap compared to the Battle of Bloomington.

Every veteran has spent a lot of time in the service griping about one thing or another. It wasn't hard for the G.I. to find things to gripe about; but on their arrival at what first was a mud-covered swamp over on Tenth Street they found plenty of added material.

The first thing that became noticeable to most Woodlawn veterans was that every time they looked at the water bucket it was always empty. The damn thing seemed to spring leaks, and a lot of hardened heroes got milkmaid knees carrying the old bucket to and from the well. With a water bucket, dishpan, tea kettle, and garbage pail in one hand and an economics book in another, the men around the trailer city started getting confused as to what they were majoring in.

Plenty of G.I.'s had a hundred hours or more in Garbage Disposal 101z, but most of them seemed to be majoring in babies. It didn't take more than a couple weeks for the vets to find that more things than bombs could give them battle fatigue. About the time they settled down to write a couple back themes in English 101a or figure out Boyle's "Theory of Expansion" some stray baby across the way would think it was a good night to get the colic, and by the end of the evening they would have gladly strangled either the baby or Boyle.

It wasn't only the babies that gave the boys a hard time over in Trailer Town, but along toward Spring a couple of platoons of rats got on the loose and decided it was about time to move in. If listening for German patrols was nerve racking, the vets found listening to rats gnaw up through the floors wasn't exactly soothing.

Some of the boys started talking of the good old days "way back when" all they had to worry about was first sergeants and K.P.; but despite the rats and babies, the boys bore up under the strain, and if you walk by the trailer camp today you can see the diapers of Woodlawn babies still bravely waving in the breeze....

The boys aren't living in luxury, or even comfort, but most of them feel the privations are worth it.

From *The Date*, November 1946, 14.

Yank on Bloomington Square

BY HARGIS WESTERFIELD[4]

Hollow-eyed Yank in a limestone crouch
Lobbing grenades on Bloomington Square,
Lifting up scared with the bomb
And the look you have hurling them
Into the hell of a pillbox before you;
The automatic fire blazes back at you:
It is hard for a New Guinea man
To walk again on Bloomington Square
Without slipping back into limestone
Lying pinned under machine-gun fire:
The limestone falls away from the live wrist:
This is a live hand sun-reddened and ripped
With the jungle, in rain-rotted battle
Fatigues; this is a live bomb
That detonates when you lift up
To throw with the flesh of your face
Hardened to that red automatic fire.

But today you can walk back home
From New Guinea; you can leave behind you
The Yank in limestone, a mellow silhouette
Already dark against a cloud-flecked
Sunset: romance of war; our dead
Don't smell any more in Bloomington.
You can go about your work;
The act stands on the Square in limestone;
The Act is in stone today.

From *Folio* XII:3 (1947), 26–27.

1. "Small Town Hippie Comics," art by R. T. Reece, *The Spectator* 7, October 1969, 2.

A Block Away from There
An Imitation of Frank O'Hara's A Step Away from There

BY ERIN CHAPMAN

It is a summer afternoon so I wander
past the Jordan for a walk among the
unsunned trees. First down the path where
the bronze professors rust, and watch
frustrated as students chat and pass,
their books stealing rides on their piggy-
backs. Off to see Nick or Roy to
kill the week's buzz with Bud, or to drink
in the light, I guess. Then onto the
avenue where the cups beg me to fill
them and their owners, while bicycles
ride their people past the night-
time hideouts, as the sun bows
to meet the gates. I stop
as windows shop and boast
of bargains and dresses. There
are children tagging in the grass.
                              On
to People's Park, where the smoke
veils the non-smoking sign, and behind
a violin fills his hat with quarters. A
bearded Man in an aviator mask
sits on a bench listlessly stroking.
A tall college girl bends: he lingers
his hand on his beard. Everything
suddenly whistles. It is 6:10 of
a Friday.

    Neon at twilight is
a great design, as Jonathan Adler would
write, as are streetlamps in the day.
I stop for a sandwich at BLOOMINGTON
BAGEL COMPANY. Bill Cosby, father of
Raven-Symone, my childhood reminds.
And pink lemonade. A lady dragging news
paper rack stows plastic bags and bitten bagels
in her shopping cart.
    There are several Korean
couples on the avenue today, which
makes it pale and bright. First
Fangman died, then Heath Ledger.
Then Sydney Pollack.[5] But is the
world as full with spirit as spirit was full in them?
And one has left and one walks
past the kiosks announcing TOTALLY
MICHAEL and garage sales at Hunter
and Fess, and the Panda Express,
which they'll soon open up. I
used to think they had Jiffy
Treat there.
    A bottle of Orangina,
and back home. My heart is on my
key chain, it is *Les coquelicots* by Claude Monet.

From *Canvas* 13 (Fall 2009), 44.

Parking Lot by the Student Union

BY STEVEN JOHNSON

THAT THE RIVETS in the handicap ramp were flown in from Liaoning fourteen years ago; that the parking meter digests a quarter once dropped from a young girl's pocket in a Six Flags two states away, from pants her mother had disapproved of; that the hundred headphones dangling bring music from 1998 Mexico and 2008 Canada and 1974 Tennessee and poems; that the ants and worms under that patch's largest sycamore are stitching back the earth a child destroyed two days ago; that a girl looks at all those walking from a high window and weeps for her family's religion; that the landscaper's glove is tight on his third wedding band; that the molecules in this lamppost shrugged and blew the bulb, and its brokenness will not be noticed for four nights; that these six boys and women read texts and two of them are about love; that love had bent these grasses until the morning dew bent them more; that this newcomer walks by and wonders if he can buy a gun; that the crotch of this bike was left out and oxidizing—its owner had rushed out of town for cancer; that last winter's salt had gouged the hole heading for this skateboarder's wheel; that this bird meets its reflection with a concussion that will kill it on the weekend; that we are all in the same milk and a breath dropped by the dumpling maker weeping in Kyoto is swallowed by this young alcoholic; that there is no true name for his stellating feelings; that all this is coarse gravel, brilliant gravel, and how could anyone think to give it a Name, how could anyone think to name it?

From *Canvas*, "The Best Student Writing, 2016–17" (online: *Canvas Creative Arts Written Work '16–17*, https://imu.indiana.edu/union-board/canvas/index.html).

Frigid Venus[6]

BY GEMMA LAD

She has frozen in arched orgasm etched in stone,
Her wet spread thighs drip ice
And the spouting fish between her legs
Has stiffened: two cold fish.
Her bare proud breasts have been modestly clothed
In a bodice of white ice. When night
Draws the shades blue light subdues her
Into cool unearthly chastity and silver
The fish head, thrusting up, immobile.

From *Labyrinth* 1992, 30.

PART TWO
·Students·

Extracts from a Student's Diary, 1872

BY WILLIAM T. HICKS

William T. Hicks, born in Orangeburg, Indiana, is listed as a student but not a graduate of the university in the first volume of James Albert Woodburn's History of Indiana University *(Bloomington: Indiana University, 1940, 414). He worked as a financial agent for the university, unwinding a scheme in which endowments were being defrauded of income from land owned by the university, and later served in a group that raised funds for the construction of the Student Building (1903), now named for Frances Morgan Swain.*

In his diary, William Hicks quotes from or refers to a remarkable range of canonical literary texts and writers: the New Testament, Edmund Spenser's The Fairie Queen *(1590–96), Shakespeare's* Hamlet *(c. 1600), John Milton's* Paradise Lost *(1667), John Dryden's play* All for Love *(1677), Laurence Sterne's unusual novel* The Life and Opinions of Tristram Shandy *(1759–67), Washington Irving, and two long narrative poems by Walter Scott,* Marmion *(1808) and* The Lay of the Last Minstrel *(1805). He uses translations of quotations from the Roman writers Juvenal, Terence, and Persius that appear in essays by Joseph Addison and Richard Steele in their weekly magazine* The Spectator *(1711–14). He quotes from a speech by James Otis (1725–83), one of the agitators of the American Revolution, and from Gail Hamilton, the professional name of Mary Abigail Dodge (1833–96), who wrote antislavery and then protofeminist newspaper columns. For his performance before the Athenian Society, a literary club founded in 1830 whose members met to read papers and deliver orations to one another, he chose to read a passage from* Plain Language from Truthful James *(1870), a book by the American humorist Bret Harte. He mentions Jenny Lind, the Swedish opera singer whose spectacularly successful American tour was managed by P. T. Barnum, and he is very much taken with a lecture on free love by Theodore Tilton, a minister and very popular lecturer who was an assistant to the even more popular lecturer and clergyman Henry Ward Beecher. Tilton later unsuccessfully sued Beecher, claiming that he had committed adultery with Tilton's wife.*

In this extract, William Hicks also mentions Theophilus Wylie (1810–95), a Presbyterian minister, professor of languages and natural philosophy, and president pro tem of the university in 1853 and 1856; John Gay, briefly (1871–72) a professor of English literature; Cyrus Nutt (1814–75), a professor of Greek and mathematics and president of the university in 1860–75; and Elisha Ballantine (1809–86), a professor of mathematics and languages.

January 6

Bloomington, Indiana

Came here this eve via the Vandalia road. Stopped for two hours at Greencastle. Arrived here at three o'clock. Many of the boys had already arrived. And now I set myself down fairly tired of the frolicking world and am willing to be wedded for a while to my books.

January 7

Went this eve to the College Chapel to hear a lecture by Prof. Wylie. His subject was "Books." He went over the broad field of erudition, leaving no ground from the filthiest to the best literature untouched. Toward the end of the lecture many of the boys were inclined to sleep.

January 8

Entered College this morn. The Profs. all wore smiling faces. Our Studies for the term are Analytic Geometry, Rhetoric ... and Plato's *Apology of Socrates*.

> "For I suffer and be still;
> And come he slow, or come he fast
> It is but death who comes at last."
>
> "'Tis better to sit still at rest
> Than rise, perchance to fall." [*Marmion*, II, iv; IV, xxix]

January 9
Everything passed off quietly at College today. Everything bespoke a pleasant and prosperous term. Nothing disturbs the bosom of the placid stream as it bears us on almost unconsciously. "Errors, like straws, upon the surface flow; He who would search for pearls must dive below." —Dryden [*All for Love*, Prologue]

January 10
"The accusing spirit flew to Heaven's Chancery with the oath, blushed as he gave it in, and the Recording Angel dropped a tear upon the word as he wrote it down, and blotted it out forever." [*Tristram Shandy*, VI, 8]. R. Hewitt, the great temperance lecturer, spoke in College Chapel. Subject, "Muzzle That Dog." It was the spiciest thing we have listened to for many a day.

January 11
Was summoned before the Faculty in the case of J— vs. B—.

January 12
Went to the college again today in the case of J— vs. B—. The [Athenian] Society halls were unusually full tonight. Declaimed Bret Harte's "Truthful James." Was appointed on a committee to dispose of the old carpet now on the Athenian Hall.

January 14
Sunday School. Golden Text: If any man sin, we have an advocate with the Father Jesus Christ, the righteous. Prof. Gay lectured this eve. It being his first advent he had a full house. Went to the Christian Church tonight to hear a sermon on dancing. He argued that since there was no good in it there must necessarily be harm.

January 16
Dr. Nutt dispensed justice from the rostrum this morning to some transgressors of the law. Contempt, stubbornness and intoxication! Go in boys and come out at the little end of the stick [American idiom: to suffer significant losses].

January 17

Have not been well today, hence I have had but little fun, although there was considerable of it going on at college. Have been reading *The Lay of the Last Minstrel*. He tunes his harp and sings amazingly. That was the balmiest of England's days.

January 21

This has been the brightest day of the season. Prof. Balentine [sic] lectured. Attended Miss D—to the M. E. Church this eve. Love—torment of one, the felicity of two, and the strife and enmity of three. [Washington Irving, whose subject was not love but marriage.]

January 22

College was dull. No one seemed to know his lesson; but that is common for Monday. The city is still gay on account of the snow, as many find sleigh riding a good way to dispose of their leisure and ready cash. "They do not comprehend the nature of a promise; it has no more binding force on them than a rope of sand and they break it with a serene unconsciousness that anything is broken." [Gail Hamilton]

January 23

This evening there was a party of young ladies and gentlemen assembled for the purpose of making the new carpet for the Athenian Hall. About forty in number in the Hall. After work was completed we partook of the refreshments prepared by the committee for the entertainment of its friends. Everyone seemed to enjoy himself and wore a look which bespoke the wish that the Athenian would buy new carpets often. Athenian! May you live forever! May pure hearts cherish your name, and may you be as prosperous in the future as in the past.

January 24

My old chills of last term have condescended once again to visit me. Their return is not hailed with a smile.

> For her he hated as the hissing snake,
> And in her many troubles did most pleasure take.

Fair virgin to redeem her dear
Bring Arthur to the fight;
Who slays the Giant wounds the beast
And strips Duessa quite. [*Fairie Queen*, I, ii, viii]

January 25

Everything was dry and monotonous today as one could wish. Analytic most dreadfully hard. Everyone seemed to have an eye single to self interest alone, which goes down well, as we are most awful tired of the hazy remarks of some persons of our class.

January 26

Easy time today at college. Profs. sick. First issue of [the *Indiana Daily*] *Student* for this term comes out in a new garb. Like it much better than formerly. Sent several copies to friends. At the Philo[methean] Hall there was a joint meeting of the three [literary] societies for the purpose of electing Editors and Publishers for *Student*. Escorted Miss D— to the hall after having spent a short but very pleasant time in her parlor. Good night Corinne [first line of a song]. Declaimed one of Otis' speech before Prof. Gay.

January 27

In glistening gold and peerless precious stones
Yet her bright blazing beauty did essay
To dim the brightness of her glorious throne
As envying herself, that too exceeding show.

Inconstant man, that loved all he saw, and lusted after all that he did love. [*Fairie Queen*, I, iv]

January 28

This has been a cold day. Have spent most of the day reading Spencer's [sic] *Fairie Queen* in which I find some of the best common sense and the rarest wit. Spencer wrote from 1575–80. The "Knight of the Red Cross" and Una are the principal figures in first book. Arm thyself in peace and clothe thyself in success.

The lesser pangs can bear
Who hath endured the chief. [*Fairie Queen*, 1, vi]

January 29

Everyone at college was freezing today. Being on the committee to sell the old Athenian carpet I was therefore employed at the hall this eve as it was the time appointed for selling it. Old times are changed, old things are new and a stranger holds the Athenian floor. So it is written. Mutation is stamped on all things. The plastic mind of youth goes through many gradations nor until it has passed the chancery of heaven does it cease to change.

January 30

Did not attend college today. Stayed at home in order to take medicine to stop the everlasting chill. Calomel the dreadful though infallible remedy is by no means pleasant. Read quite a long account in the *Tribune* of the [Benjamin] Franklin statue in Printing House Square, New York City. It is well to remember him though of humble birth rose to the first position of honor, one whom kings respected for his wisdom and common people for his integrity. The name of Franklin will ever coexist with history.

January 31

This has been a very pleasant day. Everything went off nicely at college. Shall we ever forget these sunny college days? Not till the star of our destiny is set never again to rise, not till the fire of our life has smouldered to ashes. When we are forgotten here we trust even then we will delight to revert in this the bright spot of our early manhood. How mechanical we are! When one has finished, he steps aside and the space occupied by him is soon filled and so the wheel continues to roll.

February 1

The first of a new month is like the new year—a good time for vows, but how soon in the busy whirl of everyday life are they forgotten. By degrees we yield to our inclinations until at last we give up entirely and await the coming of vow making time.

February 2

This has been spent in busy preparation for the election of the Anniverserian of Athenian Society. Our party, determined not to have the election, went with the determination to stave it off, and we succeeded by wearing them out. Had a fight in the hall which was anything but honorable to the parties. 'Tis a pity that boys blessed with such privileges should abuse them thus. But opposition is a great developer and a man having no enemies is a poor devil that has no opinion of his own. And is a minion for the ambitious.

February 3

Thus ends another week. And what have we done during the last; have we made any advances toward that eminence toward which it behooves us all to bend our steps? Are we wiser and better than we were? College and its associations has a tendency to develop one's social qualities but I fear it impairs his morals. Boys unless possessed of an inflexible conscience are very apt to be led into things which will work to their disadvantage, blighting their better natures making them fit tools for the enemy of man.

February 4

This, the day that should be kept holy, has been spent with books and papers. There seems to be a greater tendency among students to forget the Sabbath than among any other class. Would that it were not so! But man is naturally depraved, and how could it otherwise be? The Rev. Treet lectured at the chapel. Subject, "The Immortality of the Soul." And the greatest beauty was that it was very short. We fear that we do not recollect our early training with regard to the Sabbath day.

February 6

Today has been one of the jolliest. The little unpleasantness between the boys on account of the fight was settled by a compromise. Several of the Franklin students arrived today, their college having bursted up. [Franklin College, in Franklin, Indiana, was founded in 1834, and whatever its troubles in 1872, it still exists.] Mrs. Haggart, a temperance lecturer, held forth in the college chapel tonight. She is an eloquent speaker and displays a good deal of ingenuity and has an inexhaustible vocabulary, deals some left-hand blows at the drug stores and stamps the rise of tobacco as tending to something worst.

February 7

It is election times and the boys are busy electioneering. Politics once were of an elevating nature, but now they have become very corrupt and contaminate all who touch them. Could all the chicanery practiced in college be made known it would startle some of the people who look on the students as a band of pure and noble youths.

February 9

This being the evening for the lecture of Theo. Tilton, the society adjourned. Subj. of lecture, "Home Sweet Home." An advocate of free love. If anyone knows why two persons should not be married, let him now make it known, or forever hold his peace. If unlawful before, it is no less afterward. Mass. has 10 causes for divorce, S. Carolina, none. One, the land of virtue, the other of harlots. France, none, Germany eleven. Prof. Gay being terribly incensed tried to reply, but the Speaker annihilated him. Guided Miss D—'s footsteps hitherward and thitherward. A rose, may it blossom forever.

February 10

Mr. Tilton delivered the best lecture I ever listened to in the chapel this morn. "The Application of the Mind." A sword too short but he advances to make the stroke. ["If your sword is too short, take one step forward": aphorism sometimes attributed to Spartans]. Man a trinity, moral, physical, and intellectual. The lily burying its roots into the earthy, rises aloft its head into the sunshine of a higher being. Eve: called on Miss M—, an old classmate and friend, a most agreeable and affable lady, genial but independent.

February 11

The day has been warm and bright, giving the sidewalks a decided inclination to cave in. Was at Sunday School. "If you suffer for righteousness sake, happy are ye" [Peter, 3:14]. Prof. Gay having announced that he would answer Mr. Tilton, a good house was consequently at chapel, but after consideration he thought he had better not say his speech on that part of the subj. Did not go to church this eve, spent part of the eve reading Milton. "Better to rule in Hell than serve in Heaven" [*Paradise Lost*, I].

February 17

There is a lull in everything today. Spent an hour or two in the college library. Jenny Lind having in youth showed signs of great musical abilities, lost her voice and all hopes of her were given up. And only by an unceasing toil did she regain it and after years of practice did she write her name on Fame's tablets. Called on Miss D— in the eve. I love woman in all her associations. It is my religion; for after an evening with a pure and uncontaminated woman I always go my way a meeker and, I trust, a better man, and no tribute which can be paid will compensate for her influence.

February 19

Have felt badly enough today. I am becoming so slothful and stupid. How my past yearns for that buoyancy which stimulated my boyhood to climb the hills in sport. They are but as yesterday, but alas are gone. And it is not fitful fancy that they were our happiest days. Then we knew not a care. Nothing disturbed us further than a broken sled or a lost ball. Our hopes had not then been blighted nor our ambitions impaired.

March 1

Have been feeling badly all day. Was very busy during the evening preparing an original for society [apparently a talk to the Athenian society] but was prevented from delivering it by the return of my old company, the chills. It does seem that I am destined to be tormented the reminder of my days, Subject of my original, "Motives," arguing that no man acts without a motive, be that as it may, good or bad.

March 2

This was public. The performance was a very credible one. Was racked all day with fever, but kept going. Called on the Dr. in the eve who told me that something worse than chills was ahold of me. He gave me some medicine and sent me to my room.

March 3

Was sick all night last and awoke with severe headache and spitting up large quantities of blood. The day has been such as is common to sick persons. Did not get out of the room all day. A lonely dreary day indeed, but I must not complain for many people are in a worse condition. Marvelous and wonderful are the workings of nature.

"In love are all ills; Suspicions, quarrels, wrongs, reconciliations, war, and peace again" [Terence, tr in *Spectator*, 15 September 1711].

"Through equal pains her peace of mind destroy,
A lover's torments gave her a spiteful joy" [Juvenal, tr in *Spectator*, 15 September 1711]

"Man delights not me
Nor woman either" [*Hamlet* II, ii]

"For yesterday was [once] tomorrow. That yesterday is gone and nothing gained. And all thy fruitless days will thus be drained; For thou hast more tomorrows yet to ask,: And will be ever to begin thy task. Who like that hindmost chariot-wheels are curst, Still to be near but never to reach the first" [Persius, tr in *Spectator*, 12 June 1712]

Here the diary breaks off until March 16, when the writer records that he is just able to be up again after "a very severe attack of pneumonia fever which came very near laying me out." On the March 22 he left Bloomington for a long convalescence at home.

From *Folio* I:1 (1936), 8–11.

The Simple but Touching Ballad of the Farmer Lad Who Changed

Fresh from the cowy fields at dawn
The husky farmer came,
With hair cut in an antique mode,
With cheeks of crimson flame;
How awkward and embarrassed then!
But now! He's not the same.

For since that day some weeks ago,
When first his foot he set
Within the Book Nook's naughty doors;
When first vampettes he met,
Believe me, children everywhere,
He's changed a lot, you bet!

And now where once was blushing face,
And rude, untutored stare,
One sees the knowing walk and look,
The manner debonair;
He's now the very knowingest
Of anybody there!

From *The Hoosier* II: 2 (1919), 37.

From *Initiation*

BY GEORGE SHIVELY

After his graduation from Indiana University, George Shively served as a volunteer ambulance driver attached to the French army during World War I. In 1920, he contributed to and edited a history of his ambulance unit during the war, and in 1926 he wrote another novel, Sabbatical Year. *After the war he began his career as an editor in a New York publishing house.*

Although most of Initiation *is set in wartime France, a reviewer in the campus magazine* The Vagabond *rejoiced that "for the first time Indiana University lives under its own name and at full length in modern fiction.... It deals with Indiana University more openly than does the University catalogue." [II: 3, 51].*

[*John Malleson's first week at the university, walking from the crush of his recently pledged fraternity with his friend Tapley on campus.*]

"I tell you what, Tap—I'm not here to be made a fool of by anybody, man or woman. But that's not the main point. I can already feel . . . Can't you feel that somehow a fellow has a lot of elbow room here, for perhaps the first time in his life? Oh, I know there're lots of fool rules about freshmen and green caps and dousing in the Jordan River and non-date nights and all that—but I mean a real chance to be his own man, to—to—find—"

"To do as you damn please, you mean?"

"No-o—not exactly. Not so much doing, as—well, *thinking* yourself out," John finished lamely. He was not satisfied with his explanation, but he knew there was something to explain.

They loafed around the Book Nook for half an hour, chatting and drinking "cokes" with other freshmen, in celebration of the Class Scrap [between first- and second-year students]. When the party broke up, John and Tapley sauntered along the Campus path to Kirkwood Hall, and round the corner to the Board Walk [see description in Don Herold's essay on p. 92] more and more slowly, under the majestic arch of the big trees.

In the deep heaven a red moon hung low, shedding over the beeches a hot translucence, like fragrance changed to light. Romance sighed and laughed in the dappled shadows on the Board Walk, seeming not of this modern day and this bashful, thunderous west; passion rather of an old, old, tranquil world, lying perhaps beyond Cathay, certainly beyond all but youth's imaginings. Beneath this moon of ancient wizardry the two boys wandered, twinging under the caress of beauty that neither knew how to greet. With speech that was desperately casual, they chopped the silence to endurable lengths; it would never do to drift voiceless into the fantastic maze. Yet even as he talked, Malleson felt the words meaningless; somewhere far beneath, strong and challenging, the stream of life was rolling on. He saw himself, pausing at the brink, half relieved and half regretful that his plunge was not yet due. Four years longer—meanwhile, here was College, her spirit incarnate in Tap and himself, her freedom in their loitering steps, her voice in the midnight chimes!

[After graduation, Malleson goes to war as an ambulance driver, is wounded, then returns to campus at commencement for a reunion with Tapley, who has lost an arm in the war, and to arrange to study law. He and Tapley walk again on the campus.]

"John, old dear, we are aging," sighed Tapley. "Already the spring of youth has forsaken our step and I, for one, wish we were heading for a guzzle of real liquor instead of trying to satisfy ourselves with unsubstantial things—such as the halo about yon little co-ed's face, for instance. Notice it, even under the mortar board?"

Malleson chuckled.

"Your work with the Britishers has made you both a tank and a poet, Tap."

"And a cripple," added Tapley, grimly. "As one has-been to another I ask you, have I any right to ask a girl to marry me? . . . It's only in the last few weeks that I've learned to fasten my neck-tie." He glanced indifferently at his empty sleeve.

"Have you got the girl?"

The other's face softened. He nodded; his voice was somber.

"For keeps—unless I play the martyr."

"Take her; take her without looking forward or back."

They walked slowly along the path that leads from Kirkwood Hall through the shady hollow past the Well House. The big trees spread their arms in indiscriminate blessing over the new-fledged graduates, with the sedate gowns and their incongruously young faces; over relaxed old grads, pathetically seeking the lost yesterdays; over an occasional hurrying professor, mild-eyed and apostolic in his unaccustomed garb of black, topped with flaunting scarlet or purple. The Campus indulged in its annual interfusion of medievalism and comfortable commonplaceness; the chimes in the Student Building competed with the chugging of Fords; the classic façade of the Library [now Franklin Hall] arose above a frieze of fluffy summer dresses; the severe Stone Seat, gift of the class of 'Umpty-Nine, supported fat men drinking lemonade; the drifting fragrance of lilacs mingled with the aroma of Prince Albert [pipe tobacco] and Lucky Strike. The chatter of youth, keen for the onset; the poised reserve of the half-spent; the autumnal watching of sad old men and women—all became one, integrated for the moment at the powerful summons of place and time.

"... Oh, I'll make a place in the world!" ... "Yes, I decided to drop business for a couple of days." ... "Wylie Hall? Yes, I remember—but now my son talks more of the Board Walk."

John and Tapley wandered about, visiting old haunts, meeting old friends, but more and more falling under the influence of that vague disappointment which is the price one pays for warming over enthusiasms that are past. It is a hopeless business: the cloth of gold runs thin and shoddy, the enchanted voices grow wearisome, the tumultuous music dies away down the wind....

Yet these are, after all, but the ephemera. And a recompense remains. Now, as never before, Malleson felt the deep, laborious heart of his college throbbing in hidden self-sacrifice; caught glimpses and echoes of her mystical devotion in the souls of the men and women who returned.

They were his people—his by a tenuous bond, perhaps, a bond easy to forget, but adequate to hold while the Chimes sounded, or voices sang "Gloriana" under the campus trees.

From *Initiation* (New York, Harcourt Brace, 1925), 81–82, 282–83.

The End of the Very First Week

BY ROSELDA ZIMMERMAN

ONE WEEK HAS passed since your mother and father sped away in the big grey Oldsmobile, leaving you standing on the curbstone, alone. They had been ready to leave for a long time, but you hadn't wanted them to go, and they hadn't wanted to leave. Good-byes had been said four times, final words of advice had been given, the family had kissed and been kissed; for ten minutes, they had been in the car and Dad had been fiddling nervously with the gears. And still you clung together; your life and theirs would be changed from the moment the car slid around the driveway and out of sight. And then Dad's hand slipped over yours and squeezed it tight; Mother tremulously kissed her hand to you from the back seat; the car growled, jerked, purred softly; and your world of dependence had gone....

For a week you have been alone in a world of strangers. Your roommate is extremely popular; she has offered to "fix you up," but, embarrassed, you have declined. People in the new world seem unfriendly, rushed, snobbish.

You have not seen a familiar face for hours, as you slump in the window seat, looking out over the shadowy campus. With the morning's mail had come your first letter from home. Your hands were cold and trembled just a little as you snatched it from the chute. You turned it over and over, devouring the handwriting, speculating as to contents, lengthening the precious moments of anticipation.

With the first words in that familiar handwriting, a rush of nostalgic tears flood your eyes.... "Frankie was hurt because you didn't stop at school to tell him goodbye again.... *The Good Earth* was fine, but we were rather disappointed with the *Lost Horizon* [movies]. . . . The cat finally had. . . . We were expecting you to write Saturday, but— . . . Don't forget your family in your busy new life, Pupchin. . . . Love—"

Reminiscent tears sting as you reread the dear rambling sentences. Sighing shakily, you walk to the washstand and dab your eyes with cold water. You stare critically in the mirror.

"Sissy," you whisper tearfully at the swollen reflection. A small red spot on your chin catches your attention. You take care of it. You meet the eye of the picture of your mother on the desk and hastily turn away. The room is dreary. Only the dresser light is burning. Your roommate's bed is unoccupied; she has been out all evening. With a little shiver, you walk out into the dimly-lighted hall. The girl in 214, whom you have met the day before, passes, a towel over her shoulder, a bar of soap in her hand. You smile and say "hollo" rather diffidently—she is a senior. She nods coldly. Down the hall she stops by an open door; you hear her shout, "Hey, you big baboon, don't tell me you're *studying*!"

The lump in your throat grows taut.

"I wish someone would call *me* a baboon," you think wistfully.

A burst of laughter issues from the closed smoker [room]. You peer in in time to hear the climax of a story and the shrieks of hilarious appreciation. Blushing furiously, you drag your way back to your room. The hall is very quiet; somewhere downstairs a piano is tinkling "Stardust." You step inside your door and close it softly. The hospital-like atmosphere makes silence seem imperative. You tiptoe to the window and lean out into the cool night. It seems as though every star in existence was out tonight, snapping against a black velvet background. A melancholy whistler passes, the click of his heels growing fainter in the distance. . . . The student building clock strikes twelve.

From *Folio* III:1 (1937), 16.

I Hate College Boys

(WRITTEN BY A DILLUSIONED FLAPPER)

I hate college boys.
They sour my disposition.
There are the Candies,
The boys with polished hair and plucked eyebrows.
They thrive on coca colas, blue-checkered vests and three-pound shoes.
Their headquarters are the side stalls of the Book Nook,
Where they whisper wicked tales and laugh way down in their chests,
Just like real men.
They love to put on their snappiest clothes
And dash around the campus in broken-down Fords,
There is something so Elite about it.
Their one aim in life is to gather a nasty line
To rate the "hot" dates of the campus.
Whom they cart about with an air of grand indifference.
They are the reason for the "What the Men Will Wear" column
In [the magazine] *Vanity Fair*.

II

There are the campus drunkards.
They are a sad lot.
There is a special stall for them in the Book Nook,
Where they slobber over Coca-Colas and chocolate milkshakes
With dreadful abandon.
Start them going
And they will tell you of the awful stew they were on last night,
How many bottles they killed,
And in what alley someone picked them up.
They love to assume that dazed expression of the old-time toper,
And to fall asleep in class after their name is called.

The truth is they'd die of the D.T.'s
If they smelled the cork of a whiskey bottle.
III
Then there are campus radicals.
Mencken's proteges.
Nothing suits them but that the University be torn down
And built over again
According to their ideas.
They dazzle the girls with polysyllable profundities
And sprinkle their conversation with bits of French.
Once in awhile they assemble for a literary meeting
Where they read their stuff
Right out loud.
The main idea is to keep from laughing.
They are a morbid lot with some awful complexes.
They will talk nonchalantly of committing suicide,
Just to see what it is like.
Encourage them!
IV
Don't let us forget the mainstays of the University,
Our future teachers and traveling salesmen,
The Prides of Connersville, Carlton Corners, and Rising Sun,
They are the lads to read the reference books the profs suggest
And you simply have to drive them out of the library.
They go big in the class-room,
But sic them on a date
And the yokel qualities come out pretty strong.
Their shining goal in life is a Phi Beta Kappa key,
And nothing but smallpox will make them cut a class.
If they don't draw an A out of a course,
They burst into tears.
Some of the bolder ones try to imitate the candies
And go in for baggy slickers and blinding sweaters.
They remind you of a cow in ladies lingerie.
But never mind,
Some day they'll be the big men of this country.

I Hate College Boys,
They sour my disposition.

I Love College Girls

(WRITTEN BY A DILLUSIONED CANDY)

I love college girls,
They grate on my nerves;
There are the flappers—
The girls with bloody lips and dirty necks;
They exist on pink teas, key-hole scandals and form-fitting sweaters.
Their refuge is the other side-stalls of the Book Nook,
Where they coo rotten stories about the other girls and giggle
Way up in their oesophagi just like ladies.
They insist upon wearing outrageous clothes,
And neck around the town in broken-down Fords.
There is something so refined about them.
Their one aim in life is to hand out the bunk,
And rope in the unsuspecting Sigma Delta Chi [honorary journalism fraternity] sheiks
Whom they flaunt to the rest with utter snobbishness.
They are the reason for the "What every woman should know" chapters
In hygiene books.

II.

There are the gold-diggers.
This species never have enough to eat or wear.
They have never seen the movies at the Princess or the Indiana.
They never eat enough at home.
If they can't eat it they put it in their pockets;
They have large pockets.
They eat grapefruit, watermelon, and ham sandwiches as hors d'oeuvres,
But in an indirect manner,
From table to lap to mouth.

They take in all fraternity dances,
But they never heard of a return date.
The truth is this species would die out
If it wasn't for chocolate milk and maraschino cherries.

III.

Then there are the intellectual ignoramuses—
The history majors.
They can tell you the color of Napoleon's white horse
Or when the War of 1812 was fought.
They are artistic.
They color maps;
They care nothing for expense.
They wear the chairs out in the library,
They have stringy hair, wear thick glasses and cotton stockings,
But they drink listerine to hide their cigarette breath.
They are the teachers' pets.
They ought to be in cages.

IV.

But don't let us forget the mainstays of femininity,
The trailing Arbuti.
Baby-talk is their forte.
Their eyes are so winsome, their smile so sweet,
That one would like to change their physiognomies with a custard pie.
They read sweet passionate love stories,
The book in one hand, a lollypop in the other,
And devour them both ardently.
They talk so sensibly, saying—
"I'm only thix............... Ain't I coote?"
And "I'm goina keel yu"....
I wish th' Hell they would,
But never mind,
Someday they will.
I love college girls—
They grate upon my nerves.

From *The Vagabond* II:1 (1924), 63–66.

The College Student: Juvenile Sophisticate

BY NATHAN DAVIS

Although the point of this essay is that male Indiana undergraduates are too juvenile or ignorant to indulge in the refined pleasures the writer describes, he and the editor of The Vagabond, *John Johnson, were expelled from the university for its publication, apparently for just knowing and writing about how and where young men might amuse themselves.*

Is it a bit disturbing to think that the attractive young bloods who spend their leisure hours at college may be as virginal as the future young schoolmarms in the Schools of Education? Yet, whether it be disturbing or not, it is at any rate pathetic that there is any young man of twenty-one or thereabouts still uninitiated into the festivities of Priapus and the caverns of Phigalia.[2] But so it is with one type of college student, he whom the blue-stocking reformer denounces as what the redoubtable Mencken would call a perambulating six-foot phallus. Perhaps we go a bit too far; perhaps this young man is not typical. But if he is not typical, he is certainly common, and but a step removed from the young man who really is the average, and who, though not being in the ridiculous state of the former, is nevertheless much more humorous. He regards himself as "sophisticated," and therein lies the reason for many and loud guffaws.

And toward the other colossal evil, which along with sex is reported to gild the young collegiate lilies of the land—the worship of Bacchus—the typical college student's attitude is exactly the same. Such students' idea of vice is very ludicrous. It is very amusing to see prevalent among them such archaic notions as that sophistication consists of paying from nineteen to two hundred and nine visits in one year to what in the nineties was known as a "sportin' house" and of knowing that one shouldn't drink orange juice and alcohol together because hydrochloric acid is formed. And if there happens to be anyone who has been on intimate terms with one of the high school scuds [promiscuous women] back in the home village, why he is regarded as a sort of super Beau Nash. If one has done all this and possesses certain social graces, he conforms to the idea of sophistication prevalent in the colleges today.

How droll! No one seems to realize that the first of these achievements might be accomplished by any corner newsboy, granting of course that all financial and biological difficulties could be overcome. As for the art of drinking, the fact that the college student will drink undiluted gin is enough to convince any true connoisseur of liqueur of his asininity and verdancy; for who is there among the initiated who does not know that straight gin as a drink is to be used only to poison the neighbor's cat? But the college "sophisticate" will have none of this; gin to him is a delightful beverage, and all that he knows of such delicacies as Creme de Menthes, dry Martinis or Johnnie Walkers is exactly equivalent to what he knows concerning the music of Bach, the painting of El Greco, or the works of Gogol.

II.

"Pleasure," wrote Remy de Gourmont, "is a human creation, a delicate art, to which as for music and painting, only a few are apt." In such manner is the circle of the truly sophisticated very select, and the average college student may never be a member; for knowledge of the best or the cheapest (the two are not always distinct) house of prostitution in Hamilton, Ohio, ability to perform the latest dance steps, and information as to the bootlegger in Lexington, Ky. who may be relied upon to deliver the stuff right to the front door, will not admit one to membership. But the chap who regularly parks his posterior on a bench five days of every week and listens to learned savants lecture on the Faerie Queene, or the law of falling bodies, or Behaviorism, is a smug fellow, especially if he has, on week-ends when relieved from the tedium of an undergraduate's existence, undergone such experience so as to be the possessor of some degree of information concerning the cocottes and their kin; he feels quite justified in calling himself one fast fellow. "I," he says to himself, "am sophisticated."

The vogue of such "sophisticates" upon the campus seems even more ludicrous when one hears the indignant outcries of those who still believe in those curious humbugs called "ideals." These pillars of society commonly assert that the college student is usually but a step removed from total moral degeneracy. They never seem to realize that in such matters the college student is but little more than a yokel and that his intelligence and higher sensibilities are usually so undeveloped that his degeneracy is merely that of the most obvious sort. There is nothing of the pagan knight in his makeup; on the contrary, he is but as a court buffoon. Toward that part of life which is the color of purple, he approaches either with the clumsiness of a farmer or the ignorance of a high school teacher, and never with the heightened delicacy of the artist or even the analytical observation of the scientist. Again, let the truth be repeated, he is a very innocent fellow.

III.

Such a portrait of the college student may be surprising to some, particularly to those who have read and heard much of the decadence of contemporary student-bodies: of their Rabelaisian orgies on special trains to football games; of seductions of chaste and innocent young Freshman girls upon the lawns surrounding the houses of the Presidents of the Universities; of the same act repeated with more practiced girls in the tonneaus of Cadillacs, Buicks, and Fords; and of studying at nights with a bottle of good old pre-war Cummins whiskey at the plugging student's side. Whether such stories begin in the pulpit, the poolroom, or at the bridge table, they are almost without exception untrue, if for no other reason than that the college student is either too fearful or too ignorant to do anything of the sort. Once in a while there will be a man student expelled for pursuance of too intimate a relationship with a girl, or a woman student because she happens to take one drink too many. Such incidents are exceptional. For there is too much fear and ignorance embedded in the college student's psychology.

By this is not meant fear of rules alone. One might almost say that the rules made for the benefit of the morals of student-bodies might be rescinded and conditions would still remain the same. No, it is not exactly regulations and Deans that keep the campus from becoming a Gomorrah; it may rather be diverse and seemingly insignificant details. Lack of opportunity and place, ignorance concerning satisfactory methods of contraception, belief in church dogma and the superstition of "sin" are a few of the reasons why there are not a great many liaisons formed between college men and co-eds. Living conditions have a great deal to do with the matter. And there is the added reason that the college student is the sort of gaffer whose sexual desires are easily sublimated by the process of what is known as necking, a sort of restrained form of copulation. And a further reason for the purity of American campus life is the fact that as a lover, the college student if but a shade less ridiculous than the average adult American, the Rotarian Romeo, at whose antics and ineptitudes in the art of love it has become a commonplace to laugh. We may as well expect a typical college student to give a synopsis of Nietzsche's *"Jenseits von Gut und Böse"* [*Beyond Good and Evil*] as to expect him to seduce a girl.

IV.

Do we lament such conditions? Not at all. For we realize that they are not confined to college students, but are true of the greater part of mankind. For Gourmont was never more correct than when he wrote that true pleasure, like art, is for the few. Not being of the elect, the average college student never becomes sophisticated. He is characterized by an inherent lack of intelligence and of higher sensibilities.

There are a few possessed of these qualities, who are still restrained by other reasons, at the bottom of which is usually fear. Sophistication of the genuine sort—and need we tell exactly what it is?—is reserved for an aristocracy. It is very much like great art. The swinish multitudes have no appreciation of art; is there any reason then why there should be in them an appreciation of the higher forms of sensuous pleasure? It is as hopeless to lament this fact as it is to lament the fact that the masses do not enjoy grand opera. It is hopeless to attempt any change, and who among the intelligent wishes to be a reformer anyway? And so just as long as the college student prefers the moving picture to "Candida," or Maxfield Parrish to Rockwell Kent, or Edith M. Hull to Joseph Conrad; so long will it be silly to think him capable of preferring the rich shadings of the colors and hues of life to the obvious reds and green and black.[3]

From *The Vagabond* II:1 (1924), 63–66.

Woiking Goil

ELIZABETH FLORA POTTS

"NO KIDDIN', BABY?"

"No kiddin'. Dad says he can send me, if I find work to help myself some. Oh, Binks, I'm so thrilled I feel like laughing and crying at the same time!" Her voice broke, huskily.

"Yeah," said Binks, "I feel the same way. Gee, Chris (for Christabell), think of the dances and things. You and me and college. Sounds good to Binksie."

"But, honey; there'll be an awful lot of Miss Americas and things in that bunch of coeds."

"Yes, and plenty of no-good shieks hangin' around, too; but we'll always love just us and nobody else—hmmm, Baby? 'Yes' means I get a kiss."

"Oh yes!" The words were sharp and ecstatic, as if she were afraid to believe the things he said, but somehow did believe them anyway.

The air in the restaurant was blue and pungent with the smoke of many cigarettes. Waitresses moved through the haze swiftly, carrying trays of food or stacks of used dishes. The "Frosh Hop," the big informal mixer, was just over and the place was brilliant with the coeds' smart clothes, and noisy with orders for everything from ginger ale to toasted cheese. She had danced all night.

There was only one couple in the booth: a boy wearing a gold and enamel pin on his lapel, and a girl with a similar pin fastened over her left breast. The two were laughing intimately.

"Hello, Binks," she said, dully.

"Huh? Oh, hello Chris." The patronizing tone was all too evident.

The girl took their orders and went away. Binks' voice followed her. "Who? Her? Oh, yeah, she's from my home town. Used to help the mater around the house. Odd jobs and things."

Chris was amazed, then she remembered that she had helped his mother get ready for his birthday dance last summer. Odd jobs—ha! What a laugh!

She laughed again, bitterly, when she found a dime tip under Binks' plate; and she brushed it off the table and kicked it back next to the wall under a heap of burnt matches and cigarette stubs.

The four-twelve was five minutes late the next morning. Chris paced the platform nervously, waiting for it. Through his thick lenses, the ticket agent watched her curiously.

"Crazy," he thought. "Laughed like an idiot when I told her I didn't know where 'home' was, and nearly snapped my head off when she said 'Glenville!' I wonder why she told me not to be a dam' fool when I asked if she wanted a round trip ticket?"

From *The Bored Walk* II:1 (1931), 13. In this issue, every contribution was signed with the last name Potts. This story, unusual because it is about a working-class student, is by Elizabeth Flora.

Won'erful Nell

BY FRANK SMITH

I HEARD HER first on one of those not very memorable occasions—the opening of the college year. But there was something so genuine in her soft voice and her instinctive gesture that I picked her out as one of the promising ones. In self-defense one learns not to hear the somewhat acid and shrill noise and chatter of the reluctant and the sophisticated. But it was clear that she believed in the occasion and that her "Isn't it won'erful" voiced her conviction. That word with its elided "d" remained a mannerism with her out of her folkwise speech. She was not noticeably provincial, and her use of the word was not so frequent as to dull the quaintness of it. It was so genuine, so fitting that she soon had for some of us but one name. Won'erful Nell, as we familiarly called her, was not only a cognomen or a word to be lightly known by—it was a sincere tribute to a certain enthusiasm in her.

By the chances of enrollment she was assigned to one of my sections. I liked her at once. For the first few days I thought she was another Goldie Tippical,[4] and that her eagerness was a sign of the same qualities I had so much admired in her. But gradually I saw that she was not that. It was only by a kind of generous use of the word that she could be said to have ideas. She was the child of faith, of feeling, and of wonder. She had a natural fervor that must respond to something. She might have been a martyr or a saint if the pressure to action had been continuous enough. But the little phantasmagoria of college could keep her in the active forms of wonderment. For one thing she was so strongly motor in her apprehension of things that knowledge with her was always an inclination, a leaning, a movement of her being toward the thing known. To her it seemed that a good belief or deed lay on an upper level, and that there was a felt uplift in dealing with it. And so with evil there was a lowering, a stooping, or even a debasing. She might be said to "take" an idea or a new expression into some spiritual or emotional equivalent of a hand. So that her characteristic gesture was a little hovering of the hands, a little anticipatory delight in the readiness to take what was coming. She was too delicate and too airy to give her gesture the semblance of pawing over things—a habit so disagreeably present in some persons of the motor type. She was alive without being nervous or like the cat about to pounce on its prey. She was not a day-dreamer, quietly sunk in a reverie, or seeing herself projected into a movie-like representation of life. For her life was the keen pulsing moment when what was possible to do or right to do became realized in experience. Knowing was a sort of dramatizing of the facts of life. Truly there was but one description for it. She had hit upon it in her word "won'erful."

She cared only for life—for the feel of it from moment to moment, and by a sort of instinct she cared for the wholesome and the fine. She was different from most. So many of us busy ourselves with what life looks like. We see ourselves in some position of power or honor or dignity. If we act it is to attain our dream. We cannot enjoy the moment here and now because we see ourselves as someone in another time and place. We envy, we waste the sense of living in elbowing a rival from a place where we are not. Or we toil at living as if it were a far off thing to be given as a reward sometime for something endured or suffered. But she was saved from all that. Apparently it never occurred to her that she was in competition with others, or that there were rewards for having lived, or that people were to be used, or that chances were to be calculated, and traps set and baited, or that things desirable were to be attained by fawning or by vamping. The sophisticated of that day called her green, but enough of us thought she was wonderful.

Don't imagine I am describing a type we used to call a butterfly. She had too many of the habits of the bee for that. She knew how to work—how to be busy about the needful and customary things of life. And work did not bear the primal curse of Adam upon it of being irksome and wearying.

Her attitude toward work was somewhat between that of the bee and Milton's Attendant Spirit in Comus. It was not mere habitual busyness nor of perfected righteousness. Work was experience and experience was life.

So she studied every lesson every day and remembered so large a part of it that if properly reminded by some associational process or by a train of consecutive questions by some teacher she could pass our tests. She thought all her teachers wonderful. Of course some of them were more wonderful than others. Some had the habit of slightly dramatizing their material so as to push it over to the attention of the half alert. With her tendency to think that everything said by the teachers had some of the glamour of truth and wonder upon it this method vaguely stirred her ethical sense and wakened her associational imagination even though she carried away no idea or illumination from these classroom seances. She felt that she had been caught up and placed near something of great import. Like one of old she felt that it had been good to be there. Some said that such things were inspirational, but she always with wavering hands thought it was just wonderful.

Of course, she never cheated; for that would be losing the joy of really knowing things and of doing them painstakingly for those she loved. She had never worked anyone or established a reputation by playing up hard something by chance she did know. She sat on the front row with a pure heart unsuspecting the publicans and sinners who encompassed her. She hung on the words of the instructor because it was a real joy. She smiled out of sympathetic appreciation and kindliness. She conformed to all the routine and the unthinking folk-ways of college, and her conformity was counted to her for righteousness of the intellect. She was such a "nice and good girl"—she gave such an evident support to the teacher's "efforts" that with most of us she became known as a good student. So far as the books of the registrar showed, she acquired nothing but a first-class record. Opposite her name on the report sheets is still written, with evident approval, Good, good, fine, and Very Good.

II

Slowly I began to see that she had toward education what one might call the tourist mind—that is, without being able to understand it she had a curiosity about it and an enthusiasm toward it. She believed it was a good thing, in some non-understandable way; that it was nice to plunge into the excitements and the activities of college. She belonged to the generation which was trying to escape from the cautious provincialism of her pioneer inheritance. Yet she could not emancipate herself. She had only the daring of the tourist who eagerly goes forth knowing that there is always the safe home to return to. She could not judge what she saw by the fixed home beliefs and measure it by native prejudices. Her greatest capacity in dealing with what we vaguely call thought was to believe it unquestionably if it had popular approval and did not conflict with long familiar formulas. To doubt, to question, to suppose were very dangerous procedures. She thought them so needless since one must finally come round to the old, firm, established truths. So it was that learning was to her book learning, and the method of it was learning by heart. And so it was, too, that in such a safe world of things to learn and believe she could keep up the little hovering of the soul and mind like a child about to go visiting.

She could not think that the college arrangement and its ways were not the best possible. Were there not classes and teachers and books and the daily joy of learning about things that one ought to know? If the teaching were a little dull, and remote from any human interest she thought it might be profound, or at least the way things had to be in education. But labor would conquer all things. It would all serve its purpose in the end. It was education.

Her ambition was to teach—rather certainly in the high school back home, and afterward, perhaps, some time, in the dear college where she was being educated. She did not see the pity of it—that she would only help perpetuate in others her own inability. She thought of it as service and as slightly heroic. She could see herself striving somewhat like the torch-bearer in some story she had learned, being handed the torch, striving for a brief time, and then passing on the sacred light. She thought it would be enough to flash into that brief moment of success and service and then pass.

III

As I look at it now it is strange that we did not see that she was only typical of the great majority. I suppose she had so much more fervor and response that we did not notice her lack of capacity. She could understand only the mechanical, the ritualistic, and the routine. Perhaps we never really gave her any other notion of what we were trying to do. She was so fresh and unspoiled that we liked her overmuch. She made such a response to everything we did that we never really knew how little she gained from all the possibilities that college offered. We are tempted to say that she stood in her own light, but there might have been little light.

The pathetic consequence of it is that her college life had no plot, no complication, no climax. no resolution. It seems strange that she should stand out to me across the years and the hundreds of others, so distinctly and so full of meaning—and yet she is not the heroine of anything.

She simply went back, and her neighborhood absorbed her.

The tragedy of her case—or the comedy if you can not see the other—is that we thought she was going to grow wings—and she thought she had them.

From *The Vagabond* II:4 (1925), 18–21.

2. Cover, *The Bored Walk*, art by Shannon Johnson, May 1935.

Grasping Their Hard Earned and Long Sought after Sheepskins

GRASPING THEIR HARD earned and long sought after sheepskins in fingers calloused by pen and typewriter the seniors trip blithely from the environs of their alma mater. Some will go hither and yon for waiting jobs. Others will hie themselves to the paternal threshold for—waiting—until some farsighted employer comes and begs them to ACCEPT positions. Perhaps a week—perhaps several weeks after commencement the time-honored question will arise "Now that I have it, what will I do with it?" (The diploma, of course.) In order to alleviate the possibility of any mental suffering of seniors on this score, we devote the following space to a list of practical suggestions.

1. Coat sheepskin lightly with sweetened mucilage. The result is a fly paper of the highest quality.

2. Tear strips from diploma. Make into small wads and stuff wads in ears to avoid hearing the raucous clamoring of your 5,297 creditors.

3. Using shoe-soles as patterns, cut pieces from your sheepskin. Place pieces inside shoes to keep from wearing out socks on the sidewalk.

4. Print "Apples" on back of diploma with red show-card color. Attach sign to box of Jonathans and go into business on the corner of Clunk Street and 7th Avenue.

5. Fold diploma and insert inside of hat band to make hat fit upon a possible decrease in head-size usually occurring after first interview with a prospective employer.//
6. If none of these suggestions appeal to you and you still don't know what to do with the sheepskin—give it back to the sheep.

From *The Bored Walk* III: 8 (1933), 14.

Taking Aim

BY MEREDITH MORGAN

Three city girls
feeling lost
in a two-stop light town, in
Amish country, Ohio
where we might spend four years
as the locals would say.

Wasting time between interviews,
we wandered the dusty street
looking for the turning point
that would convince us to stay.

Instead, we found an antique shop
and three glass marbles.

Losing touch with what we knew
as our cell-phones lost their signals,
simple, spherical smoothness—
one green, one red, mine blue—
anchored us to ourselves.

The town square was bordered by flags
for each of the fifty states.
Arizona was upside down
so we laughed,
not knowing that one of us would find herself
at home, or at least in school,
in that almost-desert.

Another ended up in a tiny town
just as Podunk as that Ohio village
but one state west.
And I came to the last place
I ever would have expected.

Shooter marbles,
carefully aimed,
strike their targets,
which spin out of control
and collide with others,
which nudge still more,
in an unseen domino effect.
And maybe, who knows,
maybe two of them,
the green and the blue, perhaps,
will come to rest
only a breath from the line of perfection,
from their utopia.

The game requires so much skill
that it might as well be chance.

From *Labyrinth* 2005, 21–22.

New Pens, Check

BY ADRIANA VALTIERRA

New pens, check.
New notebooks, check.
New clothes, check.
New shoes, check.
What do I want to use to decorate my walls?
Which pictures do I put in a frame?
Is my favorite stuffed animal packed?
On and on goes the list.
The list that most kids don't even think about until college.
The list that I have tweaked and perfected since age fourteen.
Freshman, new dorm, new neighbors, new school.
Nothing new to me.
Yet it's all so new.
Boarding school and college barely compare.
I'm in a whole new place.
Although I've said goodbye four times before,
packed my bags four times before,
walked into a room to live with a stranger once before,
something is very different.

Maybe I'm older, wiser.
Or maybe I'm only older.
I've made a strange place my home once before.
I cried when I left it.
It's time to start that process again.
Once again, I'm a freshman in a new dorm with new neighbors
    at a new school.

Am I a new me?
I have a new home, new friends, and a lot of new experiences waiting for me.
It's my time.
I'm at home at IU.

From *Collins Columns* August 29, 2012, 19.

The Best Time of My Life

BY MARY-KATHERINE LEMON

I'm so glad I went to college
So I could "learn" in a class of 165 people
I'm so glad I went to college
So I could hear the steroid-induced rants of my be-Sperry'd classmates
I'm so glad I went to college
So I could see self-defense class ads demand I not "become a victim" of sexual assault
I'm so glad I went to college
So I could listen to arrogant white girls provide "insight" on the habits of students of color
And hear kids from Carmel and Fishers decry things as "ghetto."
I'm so glad I went to college
So my dorm-mates could leave a wig's worth of hair in the shower drain
I'm so glad I went to college
So I could clean up everybody else's mess in the laundry room
And in the bathroom
And in the dining hall
Because Mommy never taught them how to be a functioning adult
I'm so glad I went to college
So I could re-live high school
For $20,000 a year and decades of debt

From *Collins Columns* August 29, 2012, 20.

Entirely Too Much Personal Information

BY ALLISON NEAL

It is interesting to compare the genres and origins of the texts Ms. Neal has written class papers on with those quoted or alluded to by William Hicks in his diary of 1872. Differences of kind and genre, not necessarily of quality or interest.

Spring cleaning. My room is always a disaster (the drawbacks of living in a single and having no one to hold you accountable for your bad habits), but I thought I'd clean out my computer files and pay homage to the plethora of papers I've written this school year. Side note: does anyone else have to look up what the MLA heading looks like every single time when writing a paper? Like my brain just becomes goo every single time I have to focus on formatting. Big yikes. Anyway, here are my paper titles from the last couple of semesters. Not gonna lie, most of these were written mere hours before they were due:

Sex, Disguises, and Unfaithful Men: Female Agency and Sexuality in *The Beggar's Opera* and *Fantomina*
Perfect Blue and *Tokyo Idols:* Interrogating Bodies in the Japanese Idol Industry
Co-Instructor Paper: Islamophobia, Punk, and Zines
Raw: Sexuality, Conformity, and the Taboo
Bodice Ripping and Female Fantasy: A Brief History of the Romance Novel
Mrs. Dalloway: Disrupting Conceptions of Traditional Motherhood
"The Dead": Personal and Political Antagonism[5]
Serial and *Investigation Discovery*: True Crime and Audience Engagement

Designing Media: Addressing Sexual Assault and Harassment via Mobile Apps

Amorous Amazon: The Rise of Online Self-Publishing in the Romance Genre

Online Petition Paper: Voter ID Law

From *Collins Columns*, April 4, 2019.

3. "Books That Shaped Us," cover, *Collins Columns*, art by Margaret Schnabel, February 28, 2019.

Books, Babes, and Bestsellers

BY MARGARET SCHNABEL

"HOO BOY! IS it just me, or has it been a WEEK? A real doozy?" (It's only Tuesday as I'm writing this, but I have the sneaking suspicion that this week will indeed continue to be a WEEK.)

But that is why, my beloved gnome pals, books exist: to get us through all of the days and weeks (WEEKS) and, well, years that we're bumbling around without much sense of direction.

That's probably why books feel so important to us as kids—we're still figuring out what the world is, how we fit into everything.

I read a TON as a kid, but one book definitely stands out:

"A Tree Grows in Brooklyn" [1947], by Betty Smith, which follows a girl named Francie as she grows up in New York. Reading about Francie was my first time really, vividly seeing myself in a fictional character. This might sound weird, but it also gave me an idea of what a life looks like—I never really had a concept of what existed beyond childhood until I read it.

(Honestly. I still kind of don't? This might be why I have an unusually soft spot for coming-of-age novels (+movies). On a kind-of-unrelated note: I'm also fascinated by the most mundane details of people's lives— How do you spend a day? What do you do with your time? Which sock do you put on first???—I think mostly because there's no real rhyme or reason to the way I'm living my own.)

Other books that hold a special place in my heart, in chronological order of when I read 'em:

- "The Beacon Street Girls" [2003], Annie Bryant
- "The Melting of Maggie Bean" [2007], T. R. Burns
- "The Miseducation of Cameron Post" [2012], Emily M. Danforth
- "Pilgrim at Tinker Creek" [1974], Annie Dillard
- "Catalog of Unabashed Gratitude" [2015], Ross Gay
- "Bright Dead Things" [2015], Ada Limón

What books mean a lot to you?? Does anyone else share my strange affinity for coming-of-age novels??

From *Collins Columns*, February 28, 2019.

PART THREE
·Faculty and Courses·

4. "Departments," art by George Brehm, *Arbutus*, 1903, 15.

Indiana

BY DON HEROLD

After graduating from high school in Bloomfield, Indiana, Don Herold (1913) studied for a year at the Art Institute of Chicago. Then he returned to enroll in classes on the Bloomington campus. During his undergraduate years, he wrote and drew for Arbutus *and other campus publications. After graduation, he moved to Los Angeles and later to New York as he conducted a very successful career writing and illustrating humorous books* (Our Compassionate Goldfish, *1927) and books about humor (*Humor in Advertising, *1963). In 1933, two decades after his graduation, he agreed to appear on the masthead of the campus magazine* The Bored Walk *as "Godfather" (III, 12). It seems unlikely that he actually exercised any control over the policies and content of the magazine, but the gesture suggests a respectful knowledge of a tradition of campus humor.*

I went to Indiana University because it was thirty-five miles from home, but I would have gone to the farthest university in the world if it had had Charley Sembower[1] on its English staff. And I would have gone to the smallest university in the world if it had had William Lowe Bryan for president.[2] And that's the whole story. It's the story of the paradox of the proximity and mediocrity and of the glory of Indiana for most of us. It's the old story of [Samuel Johnson's] *Rasselas* and the Blue Bird and all the other yarns of good things being near at hand, close to home.

Farmer boys and girls, and small town boys and girls, and a few from Indianapolis and other larger Indiana towns, all go to Indiana because it is near and comparatively inexpensive, or because their high school chum went there—an easy, lazy way to choose a university, but maybe about as good as any in the long run. If you find a Sembower or a Dr. Bryan (and I use these in somewhat of a symbolical sense), you have found about all that any university can offer you; and if you don't find them, you might as well go to college at a Sears Roebuck warehouse. And your chances of finding them are perhaps a shade better in a small time university than they are at a four ring circus of a university where there may be so much going on that all you get is pandemonium....

Sembower is the kind of English prof who can put you and Browning together in such a way as to take all the scare and mystery and aloofness and distance out of Browning. Or he can put you to writing about anything in life in such a way as to take all the scare and mystery and aloofness and distance out of that thing. You may write poorly of it or you may write well of it, but Sembower, above all men that I have known, can make you feel that you, face to face with any phase of life, have at least as good a break as anybody, that there is no autocracy of feeling or writing to which you are denied entry just because you are a timid boy from Bloomfield....

[One] day, in class, he happened to be talking about [Byron's] two poems, Don Juan and Childe Harold. He absentmindedly spoke several times of Don Herold. Someone, after class, told him about it and that afternoon he came down a couple of miles, almost with tears in his eyes, to apologize for embarrassing me while I had only to thank him for the publicity....

Half of Semmy's students had not the slightest idea what he was talking about in his classes; the others were enjoying the keenest hours of their intellectual lives. He was much too mystic for the masses. He would talk Keats in terms of baseball, or Shelley in terms of household dust. At examination time he passed nearly everybody because he knew that you had either got him or you hadn't, and that in either case you might as well pass on.

William Lowe Bryan, President of Indiana, is one of the grand souls of this earth, one of the smartest of living men and one of the finest writers of English prose in all the world. A lot of Indiana boys and girls go through the University and completely miss William Lowe Bryan, and I pity them.

I may dwell on these two personalities perhaps to too great length because they were, to a large extent, Indiana University to me. Other men were Indiana to other students; in almost every university there are two or more professors, I dare say, who are that university to certain students.

What I am getting at is that, to a great degree, all this comparing of universities is pure apple sauce. You take potluck at any of them, and it is partly accident whether or not you come into contact with faculty men who set you aflame.

I had plenty of pinhead profs at Indiana, and I don't imagine ten-million-dollar annual appropriations can keep them out of any university. I had a Spanish prof who meant an hour of the deepest, dank depression because he was that kind of human being, and I had others who were just inoffensive blah. There might be fewer of them in bigger, richer schools; I don't know.

But as I think back, there were torch bearers aplenty who could not have been beat at any price: Guido Stempel, fine, rare; "Dudey" Brooks, the best of all pedagogues, who gave me about the only facts that I ever remembered about anything and fired me with a capacity for some enjoyment of architecture, which has meant fun to me for many years; "Doc" Campbell, who did the same for me in music; "Doc" Eigenmann, who knew more about blind fish than anybody else in the world and who could give you a passionately romantic interest in an amoeba; Jenkins and a lot of other good ones[3]. . . .

It is no credit to the state legislature of Indiana that some of the best men stay. Indiana is one of our best and one of our worst states. It produces men like Booth Tarkington, yet it runs Tennessee a close second in toleration of arrogant ignorance. Indiana is one of the ripest states in the union for the organization of nightshirt [i.e., the Ku Klux Klan] numbskullery. It is lousy with peanut politicians who will stoop to any level to please their mythically or actually moronic voters, and one of their pet theories is that you cannot make any mistake in soaking it to higher education. Hence Indiana gets the scantiest appropriations of all the Middle West state universities, although it is the oldest state university west of the Alleghenies, having celebrated its hundredth commencement last June. The Hoosier schoolmaster is poorly paid. Indiana and Purdue combined get less money in proportion to population than any of the state universities in that section of the United States. . . .

One thing the matter with Indiana University is its perpetual habit of asking, "What's the matter with Indiana?" This has become the college yelp. It has given Indiana a sort of wallflower personality among Middle Western universities. If a person or an institution continually asks, "What's the matter with me?" it is not long until the neighbors begin to wonder what's the matter, too. It amounts to a sort of self-imposed spiritual halitosis.

Many answers are given. The state legislature. That, of course, is correct. Purdue. Indiana, in a way, is just half a state university. Girls. They ruin the football team. Bloomington. A small town. President Bryan. Not the traveling salesman type. The drinking water. There was a drought in 1842, or something like that. Too much rain. The Monon railroad. And every successive football coach. I think these things may be the very things that make Indiana fine grained and distinctive in flavor. A touch of poverty, thanks to a hidebound legislature. Purdue roughnecks segregated away off there in Lafayette. Girls. Bloomington. President Bryan—thank God he is a scholar and one of the world's finest gentlemen, instead of the cigar-chewing, button-holing type of college president. And the rain, and the damned old Monon. Who wants to go to college on the New York Central! . . .

Of one thing I am sure, and that is that Indiana does not produce an Indiana type. I do not think that Indiana shellacs any sensibilities, as would be necessary in the production of any sort of type. If anything, Indiana opens the pores. Sometimes I wish I had a Harvard mustache and a Yale swagger, if there are such things, and a well set superiority complex of some sort, but, again, I am glad I went to a school which left me a little raw and red. Maybe I catch more with some of my pores left unsealed.

It is hard not to get soft about the Indiana campus. I know of none in America which surpasses it in beauty. Indiana buildings, some good, many architecturally atrocious, have been set in a forest of fine old trees, as the real estate agents would say. No adolescent saplings these, but grand old patriarch timber to touch the souls of sensitive boys and girls. I think the really worth-while college student is a bit sad, and I feel that every campus should offer the comfort of towering trees. I am glad I did not have to go to college in a skyscraper or on a sun-baked subdivision. Romance burns best on a wooded campus. It would take a pretty generous state appropriation to offset the thrill of a stroll on the board walk from Kirkwood Hall to Forest Place[4]. . . . As I said to myself a lot of times, say I, "I like this campus," and I know every other Indiana undergraduate has had many a similar throb.

From *College Humor*, November 1929, 22–23, 130–31. Reprinted with Herold's permission by the Indiana University Bookstore in 1930.

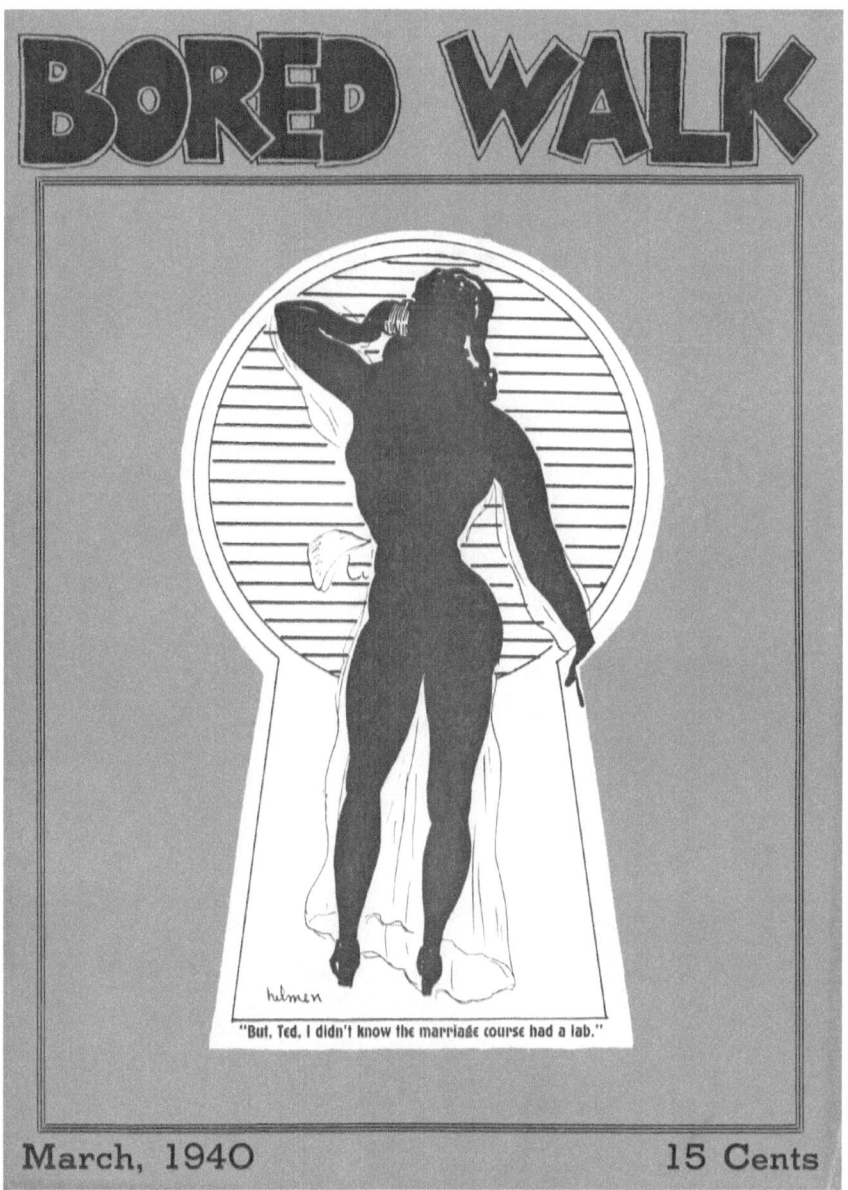

5. Cover of *The Bored Walk*, art by Normabelle Heiman, March 1940. Alfred Kinsey, professor of biology, was the lead teacher of an undergraduate team-taught course in marriage first offered in 1935. The course offered lectures on the physiology of sex and the varieties of sexual behavior. Originally, enrollment was restricted to married students, but soon that restriction was lifted and the course became very popular, enrolling hundreds of students each time it was offered.

6. "Carl Eigenmann," art in *Arbutus*, 1899, 238.

A Skinner Box[5] Named Meyer

BY WARREN BLUMENFELD

BREAK-TIME ... TIME for frivolity, companionship, and best of all, games.

"Let's play 'Pin the tail on the super-ego.'"

"No, let's play 'Button button, who's got the complex,'" said another, gleefully clapping his chubby little hands.

After lengthy deliberation, this homogenous group decided on "Blindman's extra-sensory perception" as their mode of recreation. Soon, however, they tired of their play. For a while they just sat there, looking at Rorschach blots. Then one of their number suggested they all go to the local theatre, the Von Stroheim. [Erich von Stroheim, 1885–1957, an Austrian American film director and actor who often worked on dark and naturalistic movies.]

"What now appears there?" asked one.

"Snake Pit," replied the other. [*Snake Pit* is a movie about a woman committed to a mental hospital.] And, before you could say psycho-somatic, away they went, notebooks tucked carefully under their arms, skipping through campus verbalizing their anxieties.

But perhaps I'm getting ahead of my story. Essentially these are the inside facts concerning the I.U. Department of Psychology.

Our itinerary of campus leads us along paths worn smooth by the red rubber soles of scholars long since forgotten. All these paths, incidentally, are uphill—no matter which direction you walk. Deep in the tradition-soaked, vine-covered confusion of buildings called campus is the headquarters of the Department of Psychology, Quasi-Science Hall.

Roughly speaking, Quasi-Science Hall is situated midway between Louisville and Lafayette. The last census estimated the population to be 8 full professors, 3 hungry professors, 27 grad students, 55 experimentally neurotic rats, and 11 hand-operated, semi-automatic, water-cooled Skinner boxes. The staff on hand occupies its time by confusing P101 students, breeding two-celled amoebas, giving multiple-choice examinations in which there are no correct answers, re-adjusting confused P101 students, and promoting a nickel cup of coffee at the Gables. In the off-season, each professor rewrites his textbook (thus further confusing the P101 students), tours the Bedford-Paoli circuit with his troop of reinforced rats, and contributes meager gems to "Let's Explore Your Mind."

By abusing the random-selection method of population sampling to its full absurd limit, the objective observer comes up with the following information: the average mean faculty member is helpful, trustworthy, loyal, obedient, clean, pleasant, reverent, courteous, and helps elderly rats cross mazes. He is honored, feared, respected, and broke. Sample X is well schooled in psychological psychology, relations in regard to their relative position, the psychology of psychological psychology, voodoo, social psychology, anti-social psychology, statistical analysis of statistical analysis, child's psychology of adolescents, alchemy, personal psychology, impersonal psychology, reinforcement and what it means to me (credit arranged), the rat, and the rat in his home away from his environment. The department catalogue fully covers these and any other such courses deemed pertinent.

Recognizing a member of the department is indeed a tedious, discriminatory, detailed social phenomena. From data available, however, the following should make identification relatively easy for the novice: a four-button dark green-gray suit (vest optional), glass rimmed horns, loafer-type combat boots, matching green-gray knee-length argyle stockings, Arrow shirt (quiver optional) with button-down buttons, clip-on collar, and soup-spotted clip-on to clip-on collar, gray-green bow tie which lights up in the dark and says "Psychoanalyze me in the dark, Baby."

This is generally accompanied by a Phi Beta Kappa key intellectually dangling from the lobe of the left ear horizontal to the forearm and inclined at a 45-degree angle. The eyes are extended and joined. From time to time the apparel of the psychologist will vary according to contemporary fads; but over a longer period of time, excluding extraneous variables, his wardrobe will remain constant.

However, I digress. The purpose of this bit of expository prose is to tear away the protective cloud of mystery that enshrouds Quasi-Science Hall and to expose its innermost workings to the American public. Yes, Karl K. Kampus wants to know.

There are many prominent men even now at work in the dark, dank chambers of Quasi-Science Hall, such men as Dr. M. O. T. It was Dr. M. O. T., or as he is affectionately referred to by his colleagues, "Rodney," who first labored on the concept of the effect of stimulus generalization on Indiana limestone. Fate being a fickle thing, the work of Rodney, or as he is affectionately referred to by his colleagues, "Dr. M. O. T.," went unnoticed and undiscovered until that eventful day he unintentionally allowed a section of limestone the size of a memorized memory drum plunge from the fourth floor of Quasi-Science Hall into a mob of gay, carefree business students returning to their housing units during the noon-hour rush. After that it was merely a matter of time until Dr. M. O. T. gained his present reputation.

Dr. Stan Deviation, who received so much publicity for his paper on the effects of pizza (mushrooms optional) on the satiated rat, actually made his contribution elsewhere. It was Dr. Deviation who was so instrumental in the founding of the local chapter of the psychology honorary, Psi-Cho. Psi-Cho is dedicated to the furtherance of metabolism, as the members are convinced that there is a place for metabolism in the American way of life. (EDITOR'S NOTE: In order to be eligible for initiation the undergraduate must be a psychology major and have no less than six hours of morning.) Dr. Deviation, by the way, is the author of that current bestseller, *Sane Salami Slicing: A Twentieth Century Problem.*

It has long been a tradition for the staff to convene in the departmental office immediately after lunch. Here, amid frenzied cries of "Anxiety be gone," "Long live displacement," and "Tippy-té and Stanford-Binet," the now tension-free staff proceeds to fill its paper lunch bags with water and drop them on the unsuspecting multitude below.

The entire staff faces Vienna each afternoon at 1:47 and chants in four-part harmony:

Regression, Depression, Adenoid!
Yea, Rah! Sigmund Freud!

Mad comic books are stored in the library stacks; a gin-dispenser in the rat room is used for the reinforcement of rats; the janitor is named Babinski; a cottage small is by a waterfall [line in popular song]; an autographed picture of "Dim Dom" Delieasandro's autograph [Dominic Dallassando, Chicago Cubs outfielder 1940–47], and a squash racquet once cherished by Teddy Roosevelt.

The elevator in Quasi-Science Hall, deceptively marked "Faculty use only—please use your key," is actually the site of the hottest floating Bingo game in Monroe County. (EDITOR'S NOTE: Bingo is outlawed in Monroe County by County Law 318 of 1893 which states "Curling, Jai-lai, Bingo, Kick-the-Can, or any other activities deemed immoral by the County Board, are hereafter declared illegal.") For this reason the elevator, or as it is affectionately referred to by the department, "The Shaft," is restricted to faculty use only.

Yes, this is your big story, Department of Psychology—just as it happened, just as you lived it—and why?

From *The Crimson Bull*, March 1954, 6–7.

Textbooks Unbound

BY MIKE SCHWIMMER

(A Play in 1 Act)

DRAMATIS PERSONAE
Prof. James A. Toil [James A. Work]
John W. Ashcan [John Ashton]
Harold Whitewall [Harold Whitehall]
Roy W. Cat 'n' Mouse [Roy Battenhouse]
Horst Frenzy [Horst Frenz]
Sam Screamin [Samuel Yellen]
George R. Wagonwheel [George Waggoner]
Gwendolyn Shorthand [fictional character]
Ghost of Shakespeare
Ghost of Dryden
Ghost of Milton
The Romance Quartet
(Ghosts of Byron, Keats, Shelley, and Wordsworth)

SCENE: Conference room, English Building
TIME: Lunch hour

(Professor James A. Toil, Chairman of the Department of English, has called a conference of professors to discuss vital matters pertaining to the instruction of literature at Indiana University. The conference is so vital that it had to be called during lunch hour. The professors are seated about a long, rectangular table, at the head of which is Professor Toil. Near him, pencil poised, is Gwendolyn Shorthand, a secretary, masticating a wad of Dentyne. The professors are gnawing on bits of their lunch which lies resplendent in wax paper on the conference table.)

> TOIL   Gentlemen, we have come face to face with a tremendous problem which, if not solved, will wreak havoc with the entire educational system. Nothing like this has ever happened before in the Department of English! The problem, gentlemen, is simply this the students are understanding your lectures. This cannot be tolerated!
> ASHCAN   We've tried, J. A., but students' IQs are higher these days. It's amazing how they can slash their way through the gobbledygook!
> WHITEWALL   Yes, J. A. Only the other day in Dialects, I was...
> TOIL   Dammit, Whitewall, I want no excuses! And that goes for the rest of you!
> GWEN   You want I should include the "Dammit" in the minutes, Professor Toil?
> TOIL   *No, dammit, No.* Miss Shorthand, you try my patience!
> GWEN   (sexily lowering her shoulder strap) Why don't you try mine, Proffy?
> TOIL   DAMMIT!! Let's get on with the business at hand! Gentlemen, I would appreciate any suggestions you might have to halt the growing intelligence of our students and to further confuse them.
> CAT 'N' MOUSE   In my Elizabethan Draaahma course, I constantly refer to Beaumont and Fletcher. That confuses the hell out of them.
> FRENZY   Ach, iss alvays goot to compare modern literature mit der scratchings of der prehistoric Cro-Magnon man. Und zince I am der only authority on zuch scratchings, nobody knows vhat I am spieling. Iss goot, no?
> SCREAMIN (NOISILY SUCKING THE PIMENTO OUT OF AN OLIVE)   Reference to the pre-Ovidian poets with special emphasis upon the pornographic verses of the ancient Pharaohs serves to drive students mad, I have discovered.
> WAGONWHEEL   A good book is the precious lifeblood of a master spirit. [Milton].
> TOIL   Fine, gentlemen, fine. But why, if such gems of knowledge are carried out in the classroom, do the students continue to understand you? Why, dammit, why?? (Slams fist hard upon table, sending Ashcan's lunch into the lap of Miss Shorthand.)
> GWEN   Do I take this down, sir?

WHITEWALL It seems to me, J. A., that...
(Ashcan waves his pickle wildly)
TOIL Shuddup, Whitewall, Ashcan was about to speak, and he has seniority over you!
ASHCAN I've got it, J. A., I've got it!... No, wait... it slipped my mind. I'll have it in a second.
(Gets up from table and begins pacing the floor.)
(Cat 'n' Mouse, Frenzy, and Wagonwheel whip out a deck of cards and a cribbage board. Whitewall sets himself up as chief kibitzer. Screamin continues to suck pimentoes out of olives.)
ASHCAN I've got it now, J. A.! The only way we can find out what we're doing wrong is to consult (removing his hat which he just put on in order to remove it at this point) those whose works we teach.
ALL YOU MEAN...
ASHCAN YES!! A seance!
(Miss Shorthand locks the door and begins to pull down the shades. Ashcan gets Ouija Board from the closet. All gather around the table and join hands. Screamin sucks out his last pimento.)
TOIL (In a wavering voice) Gentlemen, I feel something cold and clammy on the back of my neck! (Reaches back) Damn your pimentoes, Screamin!
FRENZY Ach, who iss dere?
GHOST OF SHAKESPEARE (Echoish) It is I, William Shakespeare. Gentlemen, I was a stupid oaf. Had no education. Had moron tendencies. Read more into me, gentlemen. Extract nonexistent philosophies. Develop ridiculous meanings.
ASHCAN Phenomenal!
TOIL Unbelievable!
WAGONWHEEL Fantastic!
SCREAMIN Eh!
(A chair squeaks. Footsteps sound.)
GHOST OF DRYDEN I am John Dryden. I was licentious, lascivious, lewd. Let's face it, gentlemen, I was just plain dirty. Tell your students of my high moral standards. Bring the religious significance out of my schmootz.
WHITEWALL Well, I swan!
CAT 'N' MOUSE How about that!
FRENZY Ich bin staunte! [astonished]
SCREAMIN Hmmm.

(Sound of a cane tapping)
GHOST OF MILTON I am John Milton. I was an irascible old cuss. I didn't give a damn for anyone but myself. I was a real stinker. Show your students how kind and benevolent I was. Point out to them my high regard for the human race, especially those of my times. Tell them how brave I was in my blindness. (Blind, hell! It was just a damn sight easier to dictate than it was to write!)
TOIL My stars!
SCREAMIN (Finally impressed) Land o' Goshen!
(Scuffling of feet)
ROMANCE QUARTET:

(To the tune of "La Cucaracha.")
We are Wordsworth, Keats, Byron, and Shelley.
Four second-rate poets were we.
Our verse in reality was smelly,
Dashed off while at 4 o'clock tea.
Find subtle interpretations.
Show intricacies of verse.
Declare it was the wealth of a nation.
For you know there was not a line worse.

CAT 'N' MOUSE What metre!
ASHCAN What subtle interpretations!
WHITEWALL What intricacy!
SCREAMIN (Unimpressed again) What trash!
(The lights go on. Miss Shorthand unlocks the door. Ashcan returns the Ouija Board to its place. All flex their cramped fingers.)
TOIL Gentlemen, how wrong we were! These literary masters have shown us the error of our ways. From now on, gentlemen, we teach only the best in literature!
ALL Horray, horray! Long live Spillane and Kinsey! All hail, Jack Woodford ! Goodnight, Mrs. Calabash! Wherever you are![6]

CURTAIN

From *The Crimson Bull,* March 1954, 14, 16–17.

The Physics-cal Side of Love

BY MYRTLE V. SCHNELLER

Oh friends, let me tell you a sad tale,
A tale that has made me ail
With an ailment most unbelievable
And definitely most grievable.

I can no longer make love.

As a premed I am excused from the draft,
As a male premed I get dates without graft,
As a junior premed I must take physics,
As a physics-taking premed I   am reduced to hyst'rics

The cause? I can no longer make love.

Last night I had a date with the loveliest of the lovely,
A most beautiful female, like one from above-ly.
We went to the show, we stopped off at the Gables,
We proceeded on to her porch, and I found I was unables

O to make love.

We sat down on a love-seat just big enough for two.
I put my arm around her—and a cold feeling grew
From the region of my heart right down to my toes;
Then it started upwards and almost froze my nose.

I realized I could no longer make love.

As musings of this sort flowed through my mind,
I thought of the magnetic attraction she had for my kind.
Magnetic attraction—unlike poles attract, we find.
And furthermore, my dipoles to hers are aligned.

O why can I no longer make love?

In form, she was, oh so luscious—
Her figure, it was divine—
Her lips, they were oh so kissable—
Her hair, it was soft and fine.

Between us there exist lines of force,
Straighter as closer we get—
Imaginary lines—theoretical—
A magnetic field is thus set.

That makes us magnetic poles;
And the closer together we move,
The greater the force of attraction,
Or so Coulomb's law would prove.

Magnetic field intensity
Equals the force in dynes
Acting upon a unit north pole
At a specified point (most times).

Now if she were the unit pole,
The specified point her lips,
What would be the force required
To bring us two to grips?

While musing thus profoundly
The maiden did arise,
Saying "I find it rather chilly—
The show was very nize."

With mouth agaped wide
I stared at the door banged tight,
Then slowly wended my homeward way
And cussed physics the rest of the night.

As long as I'm taking physics
My nights shall dateless be,
But just you wait till I'm a med
And am taking anatomy.

From *Folio* IX:3 (1944), 38–40.

A Geometry Test

BY SIEGLINDE LIM

Thirty minutes we had, to prove the theorem.
For twenty I sat staring at circles,
my inner angles frozen
when nothing came out equal.
The bisections I drew were twisted awry
while fear of the circular face of time
stiffened by blood like clock-hands,
tracing arcs I never knew existed.
Suddenly the curve stretched perpendicular
longer than any traverse line—
reaching beyond the limits of the page;
and the tallest segment of the intersected line
slit the real of infinity.
My mind was washed like a windshield, after rain
and circles glided smoothly into place,
the arcs connecting in their shrunken form.
I left that room, all theorem proven.

From *Calliope* (Winter 1994), 5.

Precipice
With apologies to Browning [Prospice]

BY JOHN W. STEIN

Fear finals?—to feel the fog in my head,
The sweat in my hand,
When the hours begin, and the nervous dread
'Round my heart like a band.
The power of the prof, the might of his pen
To fill me with woe.
The questions themselves, far out of my ken,
And yet I must go.
The term is over and the time is here.
Just one effort more!
My eyes glitter strangely while deep in my ear
I hear the blood roar.
The dance is done, the piper cries out
For that which is due,
And the glad wild days, the gay gadding about
Now bring home their rue.
But I'll take my chance—a stab in the dark—
Go down with a smile.
For all the nights wasted, each mad, midnight lark.
And laugh all the while
At the heat and the toil, the school's final blow
And its last bitter jest.
But I'll pass or be damned !—I'll write all I know,
"And with God be the rest."

From *Folio* IV:3 (1939), 10.

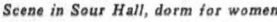

7. "25 Reasons Why You Should Attend Summer Session," ad from *The Crimson Bull*, June 1949, 31.

8. "This Is What I Do in Class," art by Emily Francisco, *Collins Columns*, February 15, 2012.

PART FOUR
· Romance ·

For Man Is a Giddy Thing

BY GRACE SMITH

THINGS HAD BEEN going badly in the laboratory all afternoon.[1] The absolute alcohol was half water, the paraffine [paraffin] sticky, the microtome [instrument to cut thin slices] razor too dull to cut. Somebody had thrown out the turtle eggs Owen had promised to save for the children at the cottage. Owen himself had spoiled half a dozen of his best slides by carefully putting cover glasses on the wrong sides and cleaning the sections off. He had then managed to spill a dish of hot paraffine over his hands. He bundled his fingers in an inky towel and leaned back gloomily.

Fortunately, Miss Gray, at the other end of the room, was busy with her drawing, and had not noticed the accident. If she had, he reflected, it would have been just like her to offer her handkerchief to tie about the burned fingers; yes, and to expect him to let her tie it on, too. Then Scott, whose special gift seemed to be in noticing all unpleasant things, would have glanced down the room with that Mephisto grin of his, just in time to see Miss Gray's sympathetic assistance. Of course, Miss Gray never had done anything like that so far, but it would be just like her. Yes, and probably she would have insisted on bringing her things over to his table, so as to help him run the sections through. Some girls never do know enough to leave a man alone.

If she had bound up his hand, Scott would have taken advantage of the occasion to stroll along, five minutes after, to hunt for a scalpel or something else he'd never lost, and to remark very casually, that Miss Gray was a mighty fine girl, a thoughtful girl; that he expected to see Owen and her at the dance Friday night; and that it was evidently getting to be quite a case. As if a man can't be nice to a girl now and then without being accused of a case! Scott's sense of humor certainly hadn't taken advantage of evolution. This thing of hearing Miss Gray's virtues sung forth forty times a day was growing tiresome.

Owen began turning the wheel of the microtome. As the slender ribbon slipped down over the knife, he reflected on the blindness that had allowed him to let Miss Gray make that Indiana pillow for him. Why had he not taken it home for his sister to embroider? Why, in the name of common sense, hadn't he remembered the Friday dance? And why—why of all things, had the girl managed—she surely had managed—to get the thing done just in time for a Friday night date? She must have worked Sundays to do it. Why had he not thought in time to make a date two weeks ago with one of the summer girls? There was that little Miss—-, that pretty little thing who had come across the lake one day with a big high school boy, and had been afraid to go within ten feet of the snake pen. Of course, he intended to pay off Miss Gray quite politely; a boat ride, perhaps, with sodas afterward, ought to make it right. The Station girls didn't expect as much as other girls, anyway.

Miss Gray, was, indeed, as Scott had repeatedly explained, a nice girl, a jolly girl; no one could deny it. Most certainly it had been kind and generous of her to make that pillow, and Owen felt that, in spite of anything Scott might say, he was not quite mean enough not to appreciate it.

It was Scott, his own roommate, who had caused all the trouble. It was Scott who had carried the elaborately embroidered red square from one end of the boarding-house porch to the other for the admiring inspection of all the boarders, while Miss Gray, absurdly happy over the affair, chatted with the youngest of the ministers. It was Scott who had suggested to Owen, when the boys first planned the dance, that it was up to him to take Miss Gray, and had made the boys believe it a matter of course that he should ask her.

The ribbon came to an end at last, and Owen went over to the pump to wash his hands. Incidentally, he glanced at Miss Gray, as she sat, quietly idle over a half-finished drawing. Her chin was tilted in her palm, her eyes half closed. Outside, dragonflies were darting about among the reeds near the shore. A few clouds rested on the horizon. The lake glittered. Not a breath of air was stirring in the laboratory. The cool water relieved the throbbing in Owen's fingers. He looked over at Miss Gray again. There she was—the same serviceable-looking girl that he had seen every day for weeks, for ages; the waist—always a white shirt waist! He strolled back to his table.

When the neurology class was called out to the afternoon lecture Scott stopped near the microtome long enough to say, in friendly undertone:

"Look here, fellow, if it doesn't make too much difference to you, I wish you'd do me a favor. You take one of the summer girls, Friday; the woods is full of them, you know, and if you're too shy to ask them, they'll ask you if you give 'em half a chance. I've a notion to look after Miss Gray myself, it she'll let me."

"Oh, you have, have you?"

Then he remembered he didn't want to take Miss Gray. He wrapped his fingers again in the towel. Suddenly it flashed upon him that this was visitors' day—that it was nearly three o'clock now. But, after all, with the Bible Conference in session at the park, the crowd was sure to be a lot of preachers who would want to prowl about the laboratory and ask absurd questions: Wasn't it warm in the laboratory sometimes? Didn't the students find it hard to study in summer? Didn't the students think vivisection cruel? Nobody that counted was likely to come on such a miserably hot day.

He had about decided that, under the circumstances, a collar was an evil not to be endured, when a vision in pink—someone very young, very pretty, very dainty, appeared from behind the bushes that bordered the road, and came up the path. Instantly he recognized the girl who had screamed with such delicious fear of the harmless gartersnakes. The very same high school boy towered awkwardly behind, carrying a white parasol.

Owen dived under the table for the lost collar, found his stray necktie in the table drawer, peeped into the tilted mirror of the dissecting microscope, forgot all about his fingers, and made himself very busy indeed, all by the time a slender girl in pink nodded shyly in at his window like a very dainty rose.

"This is visitors' day, isn't it?" she asked, with a timid little sidewise bend of her head.

He assured her that it was, and begged her to come in and let him show her around.

"Oh! how very nice of you," she smiled. "But I don't think it's so very nice in there—now, is it? Besides, I'm so afraid of the snakes, aren't you? The live ones are awful. I don't see how you handle them. I'd want gloves an inch thick, and even then—oh! it scares me just to think of it! Snakes are so horrid and the dead ones—the ones in the jars give me positive shivers. Frogs are horrid, too; don't you think so?"

Owen sympathetically discovered a hitherto unsuspected aversion to frogs. It required considerable introspection, but he succeeded.

"And what is that? Oh! A microtome? I never can remember that word. I think it's mean of the professors to have names that nobody can remember. I never could learn anything down here, with so many hard words to remember. I s'pose because I'm so stupid. You must know lots to remember such things. I don't see how you do it."

She sighed and propped her chin up in her hands so that the ruffles fell back, and looked into his face like one of Angelo's cherubs. Miss Gray could never do it that way. Owen somehow found words to assure her that he had intellectual limitations.

"Well, all I can do is dance. Can you dance?"

Owen admitted that he could dance a little. He was awkward, of course, but with a good partner he could get on fairly well.

The girl in pink simply adored dancing. So, on second thought, did he. In fact, he had begun to have a definite idea of a possible height of joy for Friday evening, when the neurology class came in. He felt that he was making a favorable impression with the sweetest summer girl on the grounds, and didn't care if every fellow in the laboratory, even Scott, observed the situation.

Someone, evidently, had observed, for Owen became distantly aware of an animated conversation behind him, regarding "the dance," and "who's going to take Owen." He felt uncomfortable that Scott's Mephisto grin must be somewhere about. Somebody began whistling "The Good Old Summer Time," and at the chorus, when the whistling rose jubilantly to the words themselves, Owen flushed.

Would she excuse him, and he would bring a cat's brain for her to see? The pink girl wished nothing so much as a cat's brain; it must be so awfully funny.

Scott, for once in his life, had apparently failed to notice things. He had come in from the lecture serenely unconscious of anything more absorbing than the neurone [neuron] theory and Miss Gray's opinions about it. At least, when Owen went back for the cat's brain, the two were deeply interested in something.

He paused a moment near Miss Gray's table, but she did not see him, and just as he was turning away he heard Scott's low tones:

"I want to see you outside after a while, Miss Gray. A little matter of Friday evening. You've probably heard about it. But let's wait until we can bolt decently."

And when Owen saw Scott looking for the laboratory assistant, he came near upsetting the formaldehyde jar.

The pink girl was interested in brains; they were awfully cute; but, really, don't you know, she couldn't understand the least thing about anything like that. She couldn't do much of anything, really, but dance. Did he ever go to dances at Warsaw? She wished she were a boy, so she could go every time they gave one. And, oh! who was that swell fellow going out the door with that girl? She wished she could meet him. The boys at the Station were so much better looking than the girls, weren't they? Of course, he wouldn't say they were, but really, you know, the girls were rather ordinary, after all; not a bit swell.

Some one behind gave a low whistle; someone giggled. Owen tried to suppress a frown and to keep his eyes away from the door. It was no use; he couldn't help seeing the white shirt-waist. He made a hasty excuse to carry the cat's brains back.

He went straight to Miss Gray.

"Excuse us, will you, Scott?" he said. "Say, Miss Gray, you know Scott's a good friend of mine, but if you don't tell him you have a date with me for Friday night, I'll never speak to him again. Will you—just as a favor to Scott? Oh, I don't care if he did hear."

For Scott was smiling.

"And, Miss Gray, it's going to be mighty fine rowing tonight."

"Just what I was going to remark," observed Scott.

Miss Gray looked at Owen, and although her face was sober, he could have sworn she smiled. After all, a girl with eyes like that doesn't need to be like a cherub.

A moment later, Owen was assuring the pink girl that he was, yes, indeed, going to the dance, and he hoped he would see her there.

"How nice of you to say so," she said. "Well, good-bye; I must be going. I've had such a lovely time. Why, gracious! Everybody else is gone!"

He nodded her a farewell. The high school boy blushed as she fluttered up to him, and solemnly dragged off his cap to Owen.

For the first time in two days Owen looked really satisfied. He was a little sorry for the high school boy, who couldn't help being young, and for the pink girl, and for Scott, who wasn't to take Miss Gray.

Near the door Scott was saying:

"I guess that wasn't much of a bolt, was it, Miss Gray?"

And Miss Gray was smiling.

From *Arbutus*, 1903, 171–176.

At the Well House

BY GILBERT SWAIM

THE OLD GRADS were returning.

Tomorrow was Commencement Day, when another graduating class would receive their diplomas from President Bryan, and then sally forth into what we call, in vague terms, Life, or the World!

Tonight they who had dabbled in the Realism of those terms—the old grads who had found success and had experienced defeat and failure, too—were coming home to their Alma Mater. Every train that drew up to the old Monon station discharged its quota of jubilant humanity.

For they were jubilant—they were glad, supremely glad, to get back once more to review the familiar scenes and to renew the friendships made in glorious under-graduate days.

There were old men with silvery hair and rotund bodies—business men, professional men, doctors, lawyers, merchants—successes—perhaps even a few failures were included, but they were all united in one common bond of fellowship and with one purpose in mind.

It was a state University; and the women were also returning, but in slightly smaller numbers. One-time-coeds, now mothers and grandmothers, hung on the arms of their consorts until the fleet of taxis had whisked them away to hotels or fraternity or sorority houses.

Finally there were those of the younger generation—those who had graduated in recent years, and in whom the memory of the Senior Siwash, the Rose Dance, and the congenial spirit of their Greek letter organizations still burned with undiminished ardour. Those are the alumni with whom we shall class Alyce Rarick and Jerry Sabin!

The girl—we shall still call Alyce a girl—descended first from the Monon coach, and then, after she had allowed her eyes to scan carefully the faces of the chattering groups that milled in and out of the station, she made her way to a taxi which was waiting at the end of the platform.

The driver looked at her questioningly as he took her grip [suitcase] and held open the door. "Where to, Miss?"

"To the Theta House," she said. As she turned to enter the cab, the light from the corner lamp post fell upon her features for a brief moment. Eight years—eight long years—had passed since Alyce Rarick had entered Indiana as a shy little freshman in the class of '21, yet somehow those years had failed to take the vivacity from her eyes or the luxurious glint from her hair. More than that, her entrance into the cab was made with the same youthful grace which characterized her movements when she had attended her first Military Ball, back in '17, with a senior!

That senior, Jerry Sabin, arrived an hour later on the next train. He alighted from the car behind a boisterous group of last year's seniors, who wise-cracked each other continually and guarded their grips with zealous care, lest the gimlet eyes of Peterson, the campus cop, should fathom their liquid contents.

No one would have recognized this Jerry Sabin as the Jerry Sabin who had so blithely donned the khaki in '17, after the never-to-be-forgotten speech of Prexy Bryan to the student body in old Assembly Hall [Assembly Hall was in the center of campus adjacent on the east to Owen Hall].

Two years in soggy trenches, and six more spent in the base hospitals of France, England, and his native land had stamped a pallor on his handsome face and had changed his hair from brown to white. The noticeable effort which he exerted in carrying his grip from the tracks to the platform would have made one wince. A slight limp and an accompanying sag in his shoulders were his souvenirs of war.

A smile—the first one in months that he had not had to force to his lips—played on his tired features as he set down his grip for a moment. Slowly and contentedly his gaze took in the happy crowds that thronged the station and the twinkling lights beyond that were the town.

"God!" he murmured to himself. "It seems good to get back again! The first time in eight years—the first time since I left! And the old place hasn't changed a bit!"

He sighed audibly, but it was a sigh of pleasure. He picked up his grip again and then, limping slightly, he walked to the end of the platform and started slowly up Third Street towards the Beta House.

The taximen besieged him on every side with their offers, "Cab, sir? Cab? Anywhere in Bloomington!"

"No, thanks!" he waved them aside with his free hand. "I'll walk!"

"I may have one leg in the grave," he muttered to himself with grim humor, "but I guess I can still walk a few blocks on the other!"

Nevertheless, those few blocks up Third Street to his fraternity house seemed like a few miles to Jerry. Painful months spent in glaring white hospital wards had not increased his endurance.

Still he was glad to get back—glad to see on his left the far-reaching lights and the ever-present gang before the Book Nook, and a little later the joyous crowds of dads and sons on the Phi Gam porch. Even the metallic plunking of a banjo that emanated from the Acacia house across the street was music to his ears, although there was possibility that the banjo was the same household relic that used to keep him awake long after midnight in the old days!

The Beta House was next. Jerry found himself wondering as to what kind of reception he would get. Of course he knew that they would be hospitable enough, but he hoped that some of the old gang—some of his old classmates—would be back to greet him.

But the sight that met his eyes as he began the ascent of the familiar stone steps forced a gasp of incredulity and astonishment from his lips and an icy sickness into his heart. Not a light gleamed in the entire house, and the feeble glow of the street lamp revealed the utter desolation of the place. The big bay windows, long since devoid of glass, stared at Jerry like dead eyes, and the yard and hedge, once kept so trim and neat by the freshmen, were now overgrown with rank weeds and littered with rubbish. A huge "For Sale" sign completed the spectacle.

Jerry experienced a cold, sinking sensation near his heart. Could it be possible that the chapter had disbanded? He wiped the clammy perspiration from his forehead and then sat down on the steps to think. It was very evident that the old house was deserted and that it had been for some time. But to think that the chapter had become inactive was too improbable! Betas had lived in that old home for so many years—no, he couldn't believe that!

Still, there was the evidence. Anything might have happened in eight years. He had had no communication from any of the brothers since when, while entering upon his long convalescent period from shell shock and gas at a Brest hospital, he had received a long letter from Tom Roseman. Good old Tom! The best buddy and the best room-mate he had ever had! Everything had been all right then, but that was in 1919!

Even Alyce (Jerry felt a sudden pang as his thoughts reverted to her) had ceased writing to him then. Of course, they had shifted him around a lot from one hospital to another, and it was possible that her letters had never found him. Jerry found consolation in that thought, but it was absurd to think that she would wait for him eight years.

"It was too much for anyone to ask of her," he thought bitterly.

"She was just a freshman, and I was a senior! Out of sight, out of mind! My God! What a homecoming!"

Jerry emitted a sigh that seemed to arise from the harassed depths of his soul. Slowly he retrieved his grip and descended the steps. As he stood on the sidewalk in the shadow of the high grass bank, undecided which way to go, a boy and a co-ed, one of the numerous "dates" on the campus that night, almost ran into him.

The girl let out a little suppressed cry, and Jerry stepped back, hat in hand. He was about to allow them to pass without further comment than an "I beg your pardon," when an idea occurred to him. He touched the boy on the shoulder.

"Pardon me just a moment," Jerry said. "Can you tell where I can find the Beta Theta Pi House, or if there is a chapter on the campus at present?"

"Sure!" replied the boy, correctly sensing Jerry's situation. "The Betas are living in a new home on East Tenth Street, across from the gym. The old house here burnt a year ago last Thanksgiving."

Jerry's relief was unbounded. "Thanks an awful lot!" he said fervently. "I'm sorry I detained you!"

"Oh, that's all right!" they chorused in unison. Jerry watched them with a queer feeling of envy and loneliness as they disappeared down the walk, their fingers interlacing.

Jerry turned abruptly and crossed the street. A path, dimly lighted by the moon and by an occasional bulb, led into a maze of similar paths that crossed and re-crossed the beautifully wooded Indiana campus. He clinched the grip handle more tightly—it seemed to be lighter now that the goal was in sight.

The row of vine-covered buildings—Biology, Science [Lindley], Kirkwood, Wylie—all mellow with age and guarded by century old trees, were old friends of Jerry's. Their presence was intensely reassuring.

Jerry stopped for a moment in front of Wylie Hall and gazed reminiscently down the drive and over the trees where the tall tower of the Student Building, with its illuminated clock dial, stood out in silhouette against the starry sky. The chimes were tolling nine o'clock.

At the sound of the bells, Jerry's eyes dropped suddenly from the tower to the old well-house, which stood half-way in the intervening space.

A flood of poignant memories assailed him then. Eight years ago that same night, after the Military Ball, he had found himself with Alyce Rarick within the cooling shadows of that same old well-house. There she had promised to wait for him forever and ever, and he, with trembling hands, had pinned his fraternity badge over her heart!

God! What he had gone through since then! He passed his hand slowly through his whitened hair and smiled, a curious, cynical little smile. They had agreed to make the well-house their rendezvous.

"Jerry, dear," she had said, "I promise I'll wait for you here every year this same night—until you come home to me!" And they had sealed that promise with a kiss.

Jerry, under the spell of the sweet memory, half started down the path towards the little eight-sided stone house. Then, with a sheepish little laugh, he halted abruptly, like a small boy caught in the jam. Viciously he grabbed his grip and pulled his soft hat down over his ears.

"Don't be a damned fool, Jerry Sabin!" he told himself bitterly. "Miracles don't happen nowadays. She must be married by this time—happily married, too!—and living miles away from Indiana!" . . .

An intense loneliness took possession of Jerry as he watched the many couples strolling arm in arm, and the occasional roadster with its youthful occupants. The full moon hung in a reddish haze over the quadrangle, and a gentle breeze quivered in his ears with the most entrancing dance music from somewhere in the distance.

He had started his "little walk" aimlessly enough, but after he had circled the campus, the old well-house seemed to draw him as a loadstone attracts a steel filing.

Hoping against hope, and with his heart beating in anticipation of an event he was sure could never take place, Jerry walked slowly down the gravel path and up the two stone steps into the cool semi-darkness of the interior.

At the sound of his step, the figure of a girl half hesitated and then arose from the stone bench. As she approached him, rather uncertainly at first, a solitary little ray of light, perhaps from the illuminated clock, crept through a chink in the stone work and gleamed for an instant on the diamond of a fraternity pin.

"Jerry!" she said.

There was a slight whistling noise, as if from a sharp intake of breath, and Jerry spoke:

"My God! Alyce!"

Incredulity, joy, happiness, love, and pathos were all blended in that last word. The two figures merged into one, and the chimes in the Student Building tower slowly and deliberately tolled out eleven o'clock!

The moon was a hazy red over the quadrangle, and the breeze, ever so slight, wafted a lazy waltz to unheeding ears.

From *The Bored Walk* II:6 (1932), 12, 20–23.

"So then I said, 'Hell, baby, you don't have to be back in your house 'till 12:30'..."

9. "So Then I Said," art by Doan Helms Jr., *The Crimson Bull*, March 1948, 5. Until the 1970s, women undergraduates who lived in dormitories or sororities were required to be in their residences by a stipulated hour each night.

Instant Idyll on the Third Floor of Ballantine Hall 2:24 P.M.

BY GARRY EMMONS

A bump and shuffle
Confusion at the door
A question of coming
And of going.
You look into my eyes
And smiled.
I
'd never seen you before.
"Hey, come back here,
Come back and fall in love with me!"
But I didn't say a word
There are rules about exposing yourself.

Come back, love,
We could fly off to . . .
To the Galapagos.
Tucked in the white sand
Like two blue turtle eggs,
We'd watch our ancestors
Creep by
And smile at Darwin's
Cleverness.
Or maybe you'd prefer the Himalayas
To consider cold heavens
And wonder why we weren't invented
Stars.
There are lots of big issues

We could deal with,
Questions of magic
And galactic inscrutability
And as to why
You just passed through my life
Like a silken bullet
While the astonished moment
Lies here bleeding.

From *Quarry* 15 (1972), 22.

Just Friends

BY TIM DOHRER

Two years ago you asked to read my newspaper,
I sat on the floor leaning sleepily against a wall
Waiting for the classroom to empty.
I had missed your entrance
But now I found myself staring at you,
Your lips hanging open from the unanswered question.
How could I refuse your pale blue eyes?
I submitted the newspaper without finishing the story.

Last year we went out drinking together and
You found great delight in my drunkenness,
Shoving shots of schnapps into my hand.
We laughed because our friends laughed,
And you held my arm as we walked;
That is until you spotted a "possibility."
Then your arm dropped away,
Leaving me and our friends to fare for ourselves.

Last night you got me out of bed.
Giggling loudly, you told me of your escapades,
Draining the town dry of every drop of beer.
You leaned heavily on my chest for support
And suddenly kissed me on the lips.
For five minutes we embraced in silence
And your hand gently caressed my back.
As we parted you whispered, "Can I stay tonight?"

Today you simply said hello in the hall.
We sat in class and I watched you
Diligently scribble notes down in your pad,
Treating me like anyone else on any other day,
But that isn't working for me.
I can't chalk this up to a drunken excuse.
Why did you tempt me past our friendship?
I trusted you and I lent you my newspaper.

From *Labyrinth*, 1990, 10.

Bloomington Lawyer

Stay

BY BETSY TANDY

It could work out fine.
An office on the square.
An apartment in town—
Four rooms, walk-up,
To call your own.
Thursdays after class meeting you for lunch
And we'd ramble down the small-town street.
Window-shopping
Thru a menagerie of faces and seasons and
Us never changing
Sedate college weekends
Blue-jeaned and hand-holding to second-run movies.
Sunday morning me fixing pancakes in the kitchen.
Two years could pass with a low, soft hum.

But Chicago—
You love that neon whore,
Her big-time glitter-eyes fascinate you

And her bony fingers know all the right places.
No dark-eyed baby could ever make you
Stay.

From *Quarry* 4 (Spring 1974), 61.

One Night Stand

BY COLLINDA TAYLOR

Two strangers walk against each other
on the sidewalk.
His buttons of public isolation
pressed into his ears,
hands in pockets,
solitary swagger.
Her backpack pulls her concentration
into the soles of her shoes
as they bump-slide over the grainy cement.
And in a moment
the right feet forward,
right shoulders pull ahead
bubbles collide
and her head tilts back
hair tangles in sweaty palms
legs twinning
as bodies writhe and fall
together
left feet step up.
And two bodies step around each other,
with shoulders squared
and keep walking.

From *Labyrinth*, 2007, 16.

Yes, These People Exist

(OVERHEARD BY: EMILY FRANCISCO)

I DON'T HAVE any quotes from the people in my classes this week, but I did hear something absolutely wonderful on the bus the other day. So, here it is.

> GUY 1   Ha. Dude, we're passing the Health Center. Wanna stop by and grab some free... you know.
>
> GUY 2   Ha ha yeah, dude. I could use some.
>
> GUY 1   Seriously?
>
> GUY 2   Yeah, man. The other weekend, I was like... "I just wanna fuck Julia."
>
> GUY 1   Yeah....
>
> GUY 2   Yeah and so she called me and I went over there. Like, I packed an overnight bag with a change of clothes and stuff like that and, like, ALL of my rubbers. It was like I wasn't really expecting anything to happen, but just in case. You know? Like, I wasn't expecting it, but if it happened, I would be ready.
>
> GUY 1   Yeah, dude. Ha.
>
> GUY 2   So then, like, we were just hanging out and talking and having a good time and then, like, her roommate, Alex, she came in and I was like, "DAMN! COCK BLOCKED!" You know, dude?
>
> GUY 1   Oh yeah, man. That's the worst.
>
> GUY 2   Yeah, like, I don't know if Julia really noticed that it happened, but it definitely did. So anyway....
>
> GUY 1   Yeah....
>
> GUY 2   So then a little later in the evening, like, we did it. And now I only have, like, three of them left. So I really do need to go get some.

GUY 1 Ha, yeah, man. Sounds like it. Maybe we'll hit it on our way back.

This actually happened . . . . yeah.

From *Collins Columns*, October 24, 2012, 25.

PART FIVE
·Protests·

Our President's Origin

While the devil was out one of his Cubs
Put some clay in a couple of tubs
He poured into each a bucket of water,
To make it as thick as jonnie cake batter.
Intending to make on the Darwinian plan
A senseless beast in the image of man.
So into the mixture a tincture of brass
And that all indispensable plenty of gass
With a lump of ignorance as big as a swine
And self-conceit to complete the design
An imp came in with a vial of deceit
And another threw in a handfull of cheat
They poured in a bottle of concentrated lie
And for stiffening a hand full of spanish fly [aphrodisiac]
And the guts of a goose to answer for brains
To counteract the sense the mixture contains
And feathers and all they threw into this
To give it that grand and peculiar hiss.
They rolled it and beat it and turned it around
Till it was as black as the coal covered ground.
They put the mixture into a big tin pan
And began to shape it somewhat like a man.
But the devil came by on his usual rounds
Said he, You imps! You devils! You hounds!
What's this? you impious detestable clowns
A billy goat, a she goat, a dog or a slut?
It's neither sais they its OLD DOC NUTT.[1]

From *The Dagger* (1875), 1.

The Ku Klux Klan Has Been on the Kampus, Is on the Kampus, and *Will Be on the Kampus*

(EXTRACT FROM THE KATALOGUE OF INDIANA UNIVERSITY FOR THE YEAR 1925–26, AFTER THE KU KLUX KLAN HAS ELECTED ALL STATE OFFICERS.)

ENTRANCE REQUIREMENTS. EACH kandidate for admission to Indiana Kollege must certify that he is a fundamentalist, believes that all of the Konstitution except the article concerning religious freedom and free speech is eternal, and must bring evidence that he has participated in the lynching of at least one Jew, Negro, or Katholic. He will also pass a physical examination as to the degree of kurvature of his nose, and the index of pigmentation of the skin. A score of 100 per cent is required on all these tests.

General Remarks. The student from a sheltered Klan family will find that Indiana Kollege is free from all false doctrines and perverting influences. Those pernicious organizations, Sigma Alpha Mu, Kappa Alpha Psi, Cosmopolitan Club, the Marquette Club, and Theta Phi Alpha have been disbanded. All Jewish, Katholic and Negro faculty members and employees have been discharged except Professor Kantor, who was allowed to remain, because his name was spelled with a K. Professors Carter, Cogshall, Coon, Conklin and Crobaugh have been dishonorably ejected, because they refused to change the initial letter of their names.

Foreign students are barred because they are un-American. In fact, the tender freshman will find all the gentle home influences. Lynching parties are held every Saturday night on top of the Well House, and after each athletic victory it is customary to burn a negro at the stake by way of celebration. In place of kap and gown the official Klan kostume will be worn at all times by students and faculty. The traditional policy of having only such konvocation speakers as would be acceptable to the Klan has been kontinued.

All books written in foreign languages have been removed from the Library, and the teaching of foreign literature is forbidden. All the writings of Einstein, Freud, Jacques Loeb, Bergson, Spinoza, Lewisohn, Disraeli, and the Old Testament are on the index prohibitus. The words of Khrist have been expurgated from the New Testament, because he was of Hebrew descent.

Official Kreed. The Kreed, to be repeated by all students in the daily pep session to be held in front of the Kollege of Kommerce (whose numbers are greatly depleted by recent measures) is as follows:

> I believe in the Ku Klux Klan, and the sovereignty of my Kleagle, my Grand Dragon and the Imperial Wizard;
> I will never fight anybody except in a mob, when masked, and by dark;
> I hate the Sheenies, the Niggers and the Papists;
> I will wear a nightshirt in public as a symbol that I work in the dark;
> I will buy my bootleg liquor only from fellow Klansmen;
> I will shun all Ko-eds who do not belong to the Klamelia;
> I will read nothing but the true Gospel, as proclaimed in the Fiery Kross and the Bloomington Advance.
> And I will keep my percentage 100 forever.

Kurrikulum. The kurrikulum has been thoroughly revised to meet the needs of progressing knowledge:

FRESHMAN YEAR	Kredit Hours
Kross Burning	5
Flag Waving	3
Lives of Great Klansmen	3
Home Ekonomiks 1: Sheet Sewing	2
English Komposition: Klan Spelling System	2

SOPHOMORE YEAR	
Khemistry 5a: The Properties of Tar and Feathers	5
History 6: The Most Skillful Jewish Massacres	3
Journalism 1: The Reporting of Rumor	2
Publik Speaking 1: The Tekhnike of Abusive Language	5

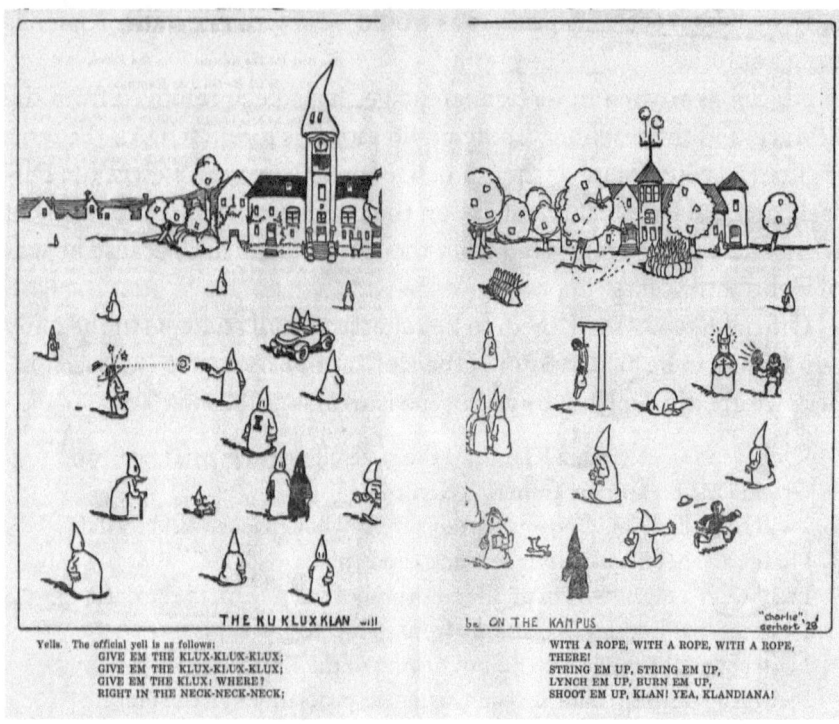

10. "The Ku Klux Klan on Kampus," art in *The Vagabond*, October 1924.

JUNIOR YEAR
Physiology 33: Effect of Torture on the Human Body 8
Politikal Science 10: The Kountry Church as an
  Instrument of Vote Buying 2
Anthropology 3: Methods of Extermination of the Lower Races 5
Psykology 7: The Psykology of Hate: Methods of
  Suppressing the Kindlier Emotions 5

SENIOR YEAR
Seminar and Research in Zoology: The Origin and
  Distribution of Kleagles and Dragons lb

From *The Vagabond* II:1 (1924), 63–66. Art by Charles Gerhart.

Dirge for the Khaki Youth

BY BOB MEYER

"THERE'S A MAN outside, Major, who wants to see you. He has a book that he thinks you should read."

"Send him away, Driscoll. You know I can't be bothered with salesmen."

"He's not a salesman, Major. He's a minister. He wants to give you the book. He says that it's a story of a man who walked about the earth teaching countries peace instead of warfare, using kind words instead of poisonous gas. He says this man can send our whole army into death and damnation if we enter another war."

"Driscoll, you fool! Get rid of him! The man is crazy. Who does he think this literary hero is, Frank Merriwell[2] or Jesus Christ?"

"Yes, Sir, that's the name he mentioned, Major—Jesus Christ."

From *The Bored Walk* XI:2 (1940), 3.

No!

BY RICHARD REED

Oh, God
I'm scared...
The paper blared—WAR
And oh, God
I'm scared.
Because I'll have to go.

I'm eighteen
And I don't want to go.
I'm eighteen.
I'm young.
I've got the world to conquer yet.
And I don't want to go stick a bayonet in someone's belly
And have red entrails squirt out all over my hand.
I'm fond of my nose.
It means something to me.
I don't want to have it blown off.
And my ear—it's always been there.
My right leg, too—
I don't want to look down
And see a shattered bone
Just above where my leg used to be.

No.
I'm eighteen.
I'm young.
Death hasn't even made a sign toward me yet.

I don't want to go.
I've a wife somewhere on this earth
And a kid somewhere out there in space.
I'm eighteen.
I haven't even begun to live yet.
I want at least a chance.
Give me a chance.
Just a chance.

I'm eighteen.
The paper blared—WAR
And oh God
I'm scared.
I don't want to go.

From *Folio* IV:4 (1939), 16.

Education or Mass Production?

BY ALBERT C. LOSCHE

I AM A tiny cog that is scheduled to be dropped off of Indiana University's streamlined assembly line in April, 1944. Once upon a time (when I was a freshman and didn't worry about [the wartime rationing of] sugar and tires and Coca Cola) I pursued what Americans call an education. Then Indiana University's War Service Plan came along.[3]

Today I also go to school.

I'm just a cussed little cog that must sacrifice what was once a precious American heritage. I must sacrifice my right to an education. In its place I must substitute mass production. Or, you may call it Indiana University's War Service Plan.

So today I am also going to school.

Today I find myself living in a baffling, revolutionary age. Every hour, every second a change in the systems that govern our society takes place. Immediately a new system, sprung from a new idea, is substituted.

The war has changed our industrial ingenuity, our agricultural importance, our labor effectiveness. Regardless of the nature of these changes, for good or for bad, for Communism or for Socialism, for people or for government, the changes are here. We must accept them. That is why I am a cog.

But as a cog I raise a question. Is this change in our method of education for our mutual benefit? Fuddely-duddely educators pat their vests and tell us that now education is running on all four cylinders. Now, at last, we are putting both college and student to work. But is our speed-up program accomplishing this?

Remember, today I am *also* going to school.

Do you think that I, as a cog, will cherish my blitzed learning? What is going to happen to me when the time comes for me to ponder and to solve those problems that were not in the textbooks; solutions that under a normal course of study could only be achieved through a liberal growth of learning, the kind of growth that I am being deprived of today?

I'm still a cog; also going to school.

Mr. Ford's Model T has nothing on Indiana University's War Service Plan graduate. Punched, crammed, drilled and bored, his pre-fabricated education will wear out when our world returns to normal and a goodly portion of native intelligence is required of its inhabitants.

Yesterday we had education. Today we have a new education—mass production.

I am still on the assembly line, also going to school.

Rush, rush, rush. Skim Shelley. Speed, speed, speed. Forget Aristotle. Hurry, hurry, hurry. Mention Shakespeare. Up at six. Peace at midnight. Oh, yes, don't you dare forget about physical education and military training. To hell with Sunday school. Ignore religion. You can remember God later: We need you now—and with an education, of course!

As a result of this, today I am also going to school.

Mr. Educator: I agree with you. This is war . . . war in its entirety, unveiled of any decency . . . just plain, un-adulterated war. We accept physical education and military training as furnishing each arm for a "V" for victory symbol. But Mr. Educator: Think of the future. We must arrive there some day. What will your student be worth then? Will he contribute toward making the shock of peace, the collapse of our world-wide economy only more brutal? Or will he accept the world's leadership and lead us into an American Century?

Give me wartime education, yes. But don't give me mass production! Accelerate on the road to victory—but, Mr. Educator, accelerate with discretion. Give me the opportunity to benefit from my most treasured asset—my education. Only then can you expect me to return your trust in that education.

Today I am just a cussed little cog, and I am also going to school.

But tomorrow all of the cussed little cogs will fall heir to the world, its troubles and its fortunes. We cannot fall short of the world's faith in our ability. We shall have no ability with the mass production system you are advocating today.

But without that system, Mr. Educator, we shall find cause to stimulate our faith in humanity; reaffirm our trust in God, and launch our American Century.

From *Folio* VIII: 1 (1942), 31–33.

Tolerance
Will It Be Future Perfect?

BY JAYNE WALPOLE

TOLERANCE IS MORE than just a word—it is an attitude of understanding. It is a belief that should have the power to grow and expand. Unfortunately, however, since tolerance is commonly connected with racial, religious or color attitudes it is fast becoming an obsolete thing.

On the opposite page is a photograph and article reprinted from the *Indianapolis Recorder*.[4] The photograph has caused much needless commotion between the *Arbutus* staff and the Arbutus Board of Control. It is NOT a shocking picture. It should not be rejected from publication. It is unusual only because of the issue made about it. It is simply a photograph of a group of Indiana women students lunching at the Union Building Grill. A group of students that have learned more than most of us the practical meaning of tolerance.

The students pictured here are members of the National Association for the Advancement of Colored People. The picture was rejected by the Arbutus Board of Control because it was not "representative of a University group activity." This is a weak and fallible excuse. The N. A. A. C. P. is a national organization for the benefit of not only college students, but for all free thinking people who have nerve enough to stand up for something they believe. It has a large membership of University students and is therefore very much a University group activity.

A university's primary purpose is to be a testing ground for future life. Supposedly all that are affiliated with a university should have the same goal ... success in college for future success after college. There are learned, well-educated professors and instructors at this University to teach the students and to guide them into the proper thinking and acting channels. A college education should offer more than just "book learning." It should help improve the growing adults' philosophy and attitude.

Prejudice is merely an outlet for feelings of superiority. We have teachers at the University to help "iron out" the "kinks" in some students' personalities resultant from over indulgence in various kinds of prejudices. This has been accomplished by some. It should at least be attempted by others.

The acknowledgment that man is a personality and not merely an economic or political unit is an important step in solving this problem. We must give all individuals a feeling of security and self-esteem.

The importance that these attributes bear upon developing a sound personality is an accepted fact. Why, then, should they be denied of any human beings?

The groups of students pictured here have the same goals. The only difference between the two groups is the fact that one group has inherited a greater opportunity to achieve their goal more quickly and easily. The other group, unfortunately, has a longer up-hill climb to achievement, due, not to a lack of ability, but to a lack of understanding on the part of many persons. It is the job of all students of democracy, whether they be white or black or yellow; whether they be Catholic, Protestant, Jewish, Buddhist or any other religious denomination, to make the results of that climb more satisfactory to all involved.

This one photograph is in itself an unimportant thing. The actions and opinions resulting from it are the things that are important. The hope that this slight piece of evidence of tolerance will help to promote a closer understanding between all students (and others affiliated with the University) is our main purpose in printing it. The hope that this one gesture will help to promote others is worth working for. We, who believe in these things, must say so. Silence in such matters is a weak weapon.

Webster, who, needless to say, knew what he was talking about, defines toleration as, "recognition of, or disposition to recognize, the right of private judgment, chiefly as to religious opinions, etc." It would be a wise step for many of us to learn the definition and to practice it accordingly. The past of tolerance has definitely been imperfect. The least we can do to overcome the past is to strive to the utmost of our powers to make tolerance in the present and future as perfect as is humanly possible.

From *The Date* (May 1946), 8–9, 28.

Concerto

BY BERNICE COHEN

I FELT WORLDS away from all earthly travesties as I sat in the Union Building lounge listening to the music of Yehudi Menuhin.

My book lay open, forgotten, as the strong strains of the recorded Paganini Concerto filled the room. I closed my eyes to shut out the sprawling scene, the lazy smoke, the clutter of crumpled cellophane in the ash trays, and even the temperamental flames in the huge grate.

As I relaxed on the couch to wait for my sister, I felt someone ease down beside me. Startled, I roused myself and leaned to remove my coat from the back. I saw then that one of the University A.S.T.P.[5] soldiers was sitting to my right. He smiled at me, a shy, friendly smile. I do not know why I looked away; I could easily have nodded in return.

Looking at him, I saw that he was a young, clean-cut fellow, one of the type that smiles out from war bond posters on bulletin boards. I watched his hands catch the rhythm of the melody and strum it on his pants leg. He must have felt my observing him, for he turned and stared. Now, I thought, I must say something.

"It's lovely, isn't it?" What else could I have said? He agreed.

"I used to play the violin," he added. His strong voice carried, and when one of the other listeners turned in annoyance, the boy made a wry face and whispered more softly,

"I've heard Jascha Heifetz in Chicago."

"Oh, you're from Chicago?" I could just as easily have asked if he liked to drink tea with preserves at the bottom. His home town was of no consequence to me; yet he seemed eager to talk.

He was from Urbana, Illinois, and he had attended the University of Chicago for seven months before he entered the army. His name was Tom

Rheeves, Rheeves with an "aitch," and his parents were strict Methodists in Urbana. Urbana and Champaign were practically the same city, and although the university at home was a good one, he had wanted to go on to Chicago, and did, he confided.

There is something about a boy's expressing all his hopes and dreams of a lifetime in five minutes. Perhaps the music helped. The record changed. Now a light, gay tune with flutes taking the melody pervaded the room. I glanced at the clock in the corner. It read 3:45. Ethel and Joel would stop for me in the lounge in a few moments. I looked at Tom Rheeves, while he fumbled for his cigarettes, and wondered why I did not leave before they came.

"Smoke?" He offered me his package. I shook my head. While he lit his cigarette, I interested myself in the two older men in khaki sitting across from us. They were conversing in some foreign tongue, using their hands freely. Tom Rheeves looked, too.

"They're language students . . . speaking Turkish, I think," he explained. "You know, I thought perhaps you were Italian or Hungarian or something."

His statement caught me off-guard. "I? Why—I—my father was dark," I countered. I should have walked out before we started on personalities. We should have stayed on the subject of Urbana. They would be here soon.

He stood up and stretched like a sleepy little boy. How about a "coke" in the Commons, he suggested. I declined. I was meeting my sister and her boyfriend in a few minutes, I told him. I wished that he would leave right away. I stood and reached for my coat. He took it from me and helped me put it on. I heard him ask about seeing me on Saturday night. His voice was miles away, for I saw Ethel and Joel, then, standing in the doorway of the lounge. How long they had been there I did not know.

The music stopped, and there was silence. Once more the Concerto began. Even the happy allegro hid jeweled tears.

I turned to Tom Rheeves and said, "Thank you," quietly. As I walked up to Ethel and linked my arm in hers, I seemed to hear the soldier's shocked gasp, and I shivered in my warm coat.

I should have told him that I was colored.

From *Folio* IX:3 (1944), 32–33.

From *The Translator*

BY JOHN CROWLEY

In 1962, the campus chapter of the Fair Play for Cuba committee and other campus peace and political organizations planned a march from the auditorium down Seventh Street to the Bloomington square to protest American policy toward Cuba and its efforts to overthrow the government of Fidel Castro. The immediate cause for the protest was the construction of sites in Cuba for the storage and launching of intercontinental missiles, supplied by the Russian government. One motive for the protest was the fear that the American government would use this provocation as a reason to destroy the Castro government; another was that the confrontation would end in nuclear war. The marchers got no farther than Indiana Avenue, where they were attacked by spectators and other students. The event can be said to mark the beginning in Bloomington of the politically turbulent 1960s.

Some of the peace and political groups participating in the march are identified in the second paragraph by initials: YSPL: Young People's Socialist League; SANE: Committee for a Sane Nuclear Policy; ADA: Americans for Democratic Action.

John Crowley (1942–) graduated from Indiana University in 1964. He has written over a dozen novels and many short stories and written scripts for and produced documentary films. He teaches writing at Yale University.

The Unitarian church was bleak and homey at once, like a school cafeteria or a basement game room. There was no cross and no colored glass and the pews were square-backed and had worn velvet cushions to sit on. It was the first church that wasn't a Catholic church that Kit had ever been in; a little shadow of trespass was only one of the new feelings she felt sitting there. She watched the people come in and the minister in a blue button-down shirt and no tie set up a microphone and folding chairs for the speakers in front of the altar.

Saul and Max and the YSPL guys registered the people who came in, got signatures from those who were willing to sign. There were people from ADA in ties or in dresses; there were two women from SANE who each wore the black button with a white figure on it that Jackie told her was the semaphore letters for N and D laid one other the other, and they stood for Nuclear Disarmament. Kit wondered how people were supposed to know this.

"So are you guys representing the Student Peace Union?" Max asked two boyish blonds, almost twins, in argyle sweaters.

"We're not representing it," one said. "We are it."

In the end the church filled and the speakers one by one got up and tapped the mike and spoke. "Don't say it's too terrible to be used," the SANE woman said. "Just because you wouldn't use it. It's not too terrible. It's been used. We used it. Eisenhower threatened to drop one on the Chinese in Korea. Just a little one. He was going to lend one to the French in Indochina. Don't tell me it's inconceivable."

"These missiles are a danger to this country," the ADA man in a tweed jacket and striped tie said. "But after all they are equivalent to our own missile bases in England and in Turkey. There has to be a general summit-level discussion on the reduction of these forces around the world. Sudden precipitate action...."

But Max had stood up in the audience, his long S shape, and started to speak. "Well these weapons may not represent a new danger to us," he said, "but we are sure a danger to Cuba. And this government would prefer Cuba to be defenseless. The Russians are lending a hand to the little kid who is about to get beat up...."

There were shouts of *No, no* and protests. Max slid his big hands into his pockets and went on. "Kennedy says we've got no plans to invade Cuba at the present time. *At the present time.* Well, swell. Must make them feel confident down there." More protests, but Max didn't raise his voice. "Kennedy's risking the end of civilization to get another whack at Castro. Do we go along? Sixty-four dollar question." [Tag line in a popular television quiz show.]

Splits and opposition appeared among the groups, an ill will spreading that Kit could only partly perceive. It was like a family argument where what someone said reminded others of everything that person always said or shouted, so that people began responding angrily at the first words, as though they knew what had to be coming. Saul took over the mike and the Fair Play for Cuba committee proposed a rationale for a march on Saturday, coordinated with the protest marches the national committee was sponsoring in Washington and at the UN. The theme of the march would be Hands Off Cuba. There was real shouting and some people walked out.

"Listen," Jackie said to Kit, leaning close. "I don't think you should get involved with this."

"I am," Kit said. "I'm here."

"I don't think that you should participate in this thing tomorrow. It's not anything that's going to do you any good."

"What do you mean? Any good?"

He looked away, at Saul going through a list and asking for volunteers, at the darkened windows, and at his hands. "I just think you ought not to," he said softly. "I can't even promise you'll be safe."

"I'm not," she said. "I'm not safe."

"Kit," Jackie said, but still he didn't look at her. "For once. Listen and believe me." . . .

No rain fell that night on the University campus, but the leaves of all the trees, yellow elms and hickory, gray-green ash, coppery oak and beech, seemed to have fallen all at once in the night: long wind-combed rows of them moving in the still-restless air, dead souls lifted and tossed on gusts.

People were in motion too. Kit crossing the campus from the College Street gate felt them, small eddies or flocks, people coming in from Fraternity Row and from town in numbers, the way they did on class days, hurrying together toward their classes in different buildings; but this wasn't a class day, and they seemed to be all going one way. She went that way too. . . .

Many people were running, or hurrying as though not to miss something. They were becoming a crowd, rivulets flowing together into a stream and flowing faster. The earth rose up a little there, between the student center and the science building, beyond which lay the central axis of the campus, a broad way starting at the auditorium and lined with the newer buildings. That's where the crowd was going, following the paths or pouring over the grass and through the leaves. Kit came to the top of the rise and saw what it was: the Fair Play for Cuba Committee and the other groups were marching, a little band with signs. Kit could just hear, like a plea repeated, the marchers' voices, and the cries and shouts of the people around them, moving with them and pressing on them, a gauntlet they passed through. There were no more than twenty or thirty of them.

She went down that way, drawn along. There was Saul Greenleaf, in the front, and Rodger in a jacket and tie and his porkpie hat. Max was in back, keeping the group together. Black and white cars of the University police were pulled up along the route, their lights revolving and their radios emitting staticky communications louder than the protestors' chants. Up on top of the auditorium Kit could see watchers and the tall tripods of cameras with long lenses, men with binoculars. . . . Jackie had said it would do her no good to be here: did he know it would be like this? Photographers scooted along the march route too, and some of them looked like news photographers, and some of them didn't.

She felt a tug at her sleeve, and pulled away, threatened. It was Fran.

"Unbelievable," she said in cold scorn. "Can you believe this?"

It seemed that in a short time the furious crowd would fall on the demonstrators and beat them or worse. Kit and Fran went down the slope, hurrying as everyone hurried.

"You can think what you want," Fran said. "You can say what you want. But this is ludicrous."

A sign that read *Hands Off Cuba* was torn from someone's hands and ripped to pieces to awful cheering.

"Who *are* these people?" Fran said. "*College students*? They're rednecks."

"Fran."

"Well you hear what they're saying? 'Commies go back to Russia.' I mean come on."

She tossed down her cigarette and stepped on it. "Dopes. Know-nothings."

They pushed through the mass of hecklers and yellers that undulated along the march route until they were at the front of the crowd and keeping pace with the marchers. And without ever exactly choosing to, they became marchers, as though sorted from the crowd by a sorter that recognized only two kinds, if you weren't one you were the other. Someone she didn't know linked arms with her. Saul saw her and grinned, amazed, alight, unafraid she thought, or maybe not. A tall athletic guy was bent into his face, speaking curses meant just for him it seemed; on the guy's crewcut head was a novelty straw hat decorated with church keys [beer can openers] and a little sign that said *Let's Raise Hell*. . . .

It was what Kit had forever most hated and feared, to be pointed at and stared at and mocked. In the Passion story when she was a kid it was this that hurt her most, that the crowds mocked Jesus and spit on him. But she felt none of that now. She could see and assess the crowd around them as though they were etched. Almost all were men, many wearing their fraternity sweatshirts and their varsity jackets, some of them though in blazers and ties, with American-flag pins in their lapels and wolfish gins, not guys who got to be part of a mob very often and seeming to enjoy it. One guy who bore down on them wore the button that the SANE women had worn, the three white lines on black, but when he came closer to Kit—so close and yelling so loud that she could see the fillings in his teeth—she saw that on his button the white lines were formed into a great swept-wing bomber, and beneath it were small letters that spelled DROP IT.

"Keep the women in the center!" Saul yelled back at this shrinking group. "Keep the women in the center, men on the outside!" The marchers had ceased their chanting, Peace Now and Hands Off Cuba; it was obvious that it just goaded the crowd dangerously, but the women who walked with Kit and Fran, arms now more protectively linked than before, started to sing. They sang, amazingly, *Dona, dona nobis, dona nobis pacem* [give us peace].

It was a round: one took up after the other had started, kept on after she ended. Fran laughed aloud, apparently she knew what they were singing, she right away began singing along in a loud hoarse voice perfectly on key, and Kit sang too when after a moment she got the tune: *Dona nobis, dona nobis, dona nobis pacem*, the women's voices cycled. . . .

"We got to break this up," [Max] said. "Somebody'll get hurt. . . . Get up and tell Saul and the people in front. We've got to break it up. Go do that."

She went back along the side of the marching group, too tightly and defensively bound together now to pass through. When she came to the front she saw that Saul was less certain too than he had been, and that ahead the opposing crowd was coming together in a wall that wouldn't let them pass. "Where's the cops?" she heard him say. "*Now* where's the cops? Free speech, people. Land of the free."

In a minute the march would not be a march any longer, it would be huddle of victims, the ones in the rear were pressing already against the slowing front rank. Almost all their signs were gone. Then just as their forward progress was about to stop altogether, Saul stepped quickly out ahead and turned to face his group, walking backward like a drum major. With both hands he waved them to the right, off the main way and onto the walks of the campus.

"Okay, *quick*!" he called out. "Keep on, keep together! We're going to end this *at the library*! Everybody hear that? Pass that on! At the library steps!" All the while waving them to the right and on. They did go faster too, almost broke into a run, and for the first time Kit felt fear, that they might run, and what might happen to them then. But they didn't, even though the crowd around gave an awful cry of rage and triumph to see that they had given up and were getting away....

The library was open. At the steps Saul and Max ushered them all inside, medieval outlaws claiming sanctuary; a few though stayed outside to deal with the crowd—Saul, whose chest was heaving maybe from the unaccustomed exercise, and Max, unperturbed, hands clasped behind his back and even smiling when Kit went by him into the dark silent inside.

For a moment she felt it had grown suddenly not dark but black, and her feet lost touch with the floor, as though it melted into liquid; then she felt someone take her arm and steady her.

"Okay?"

"Yes. Yes. Okay."

How long did they hide there? The librarian came to speak to them more than once, hushing them and telling them, which they knew, that the library was a place of study and work, not conversation and mingling. Someone was crying. Time passed. Above their heads, all around the base of the rotunda, were words printed in gold: *A Good Book Is the Precious Blood of a Master Spirit* [Milton]. The doors kept opening to show the day and admitting more of the demonstrators, and also those who had bones to pick with them, their voices dropping to hissing whispers, until the librarian chased them away too.

Kit sat huddled on the bench by the great doors where you could sit to pull off your galoshes or overshoes, which were not allowed in the halls and stacks.

"Kit," Fran said, studying her. "Are you sick?"

"I don't know."

"How long since you ate?"

"I forget." . . .

"We'll go eat," Fran said. "Hell with these people."

From *The Translator* (New York: William Morrow, 2002), 241–43, 269–64.

OH No! CRUD Strikes Again

BY GEORGE METSKY

THE SPECTATOR FOUND out late last night that CRUD is back on campus and is in the process of organizing for this year's Little 500. The following is a piece of recruitment literature which we happened to rip off from their secret files. We print this as a warning of impending trouble and hope that the proper precautions are taken.

CRUD is back. We're ready to fight the counter-revolutionaries of the Stupid [IU] Foundation once again. For all you newcomers, CRUD stands for Campus Radicals United for Destruction, and it's time that we mobilize our forces against the great Rah-Rah Conspiracy or the Bloomington 600 as we like to call them. We have the plans and we have the people to do it so be expecting a fun weekend, the second weekend in May.

First of all, CRUD has expanded this year and now has two satellite groups. They are a military arm called the Campus Radicals' Army of the People or CRAP, and a research and development group called the Concerned Liberators of Applied Plastics or CLAP.

CLAP has done a lot of work and thanks to its research we are expecting even bigger things this year. For instance, they have developed a rubber-seeking missile which we plan to use on race day. They have also perfected Ice-9 which will be used at the Regatta. (Ice-9 is capable of turning the Lake into the world's biggest ice cube within a matter of seconds.)[6] CLAP has also done research into genetic breeding and has applied its findings to moths whose use will be explained later. In all their research has been very rewarding and other examples will be cited later also.

CRAP, on the other hand, has been working on battle plans for all fronts and some of these can be seen in the diagrams contained in this article. Now however is the time to concern ourselves with the discussion of specific battles and confrontations for an elaboration of CRAP's plans and CRUD's goals.

First to be attacked will be the fascist's, oops, fashion show. CLAP's moths, which have been bred specifically for this event, will be released into the ventilation system and will devour all of the clothing within a matter of seconds. (Note: this is a concession to all of our lovers of skin—it should be a good day for all of you who enjoy viewing the human body.)

The regatta is next in line to meet the savage fury of CRUD. . . . Nothing is going to be left to chance. The area will be heavily saturated with mines and other explosives. If for some reason these fail to stop the race, a CRUD plane will drop Ice-9 into the Lake itself. The concession stands will be run by the members of CRUD and the food served will be treated so as to guarantee a freaky time for all.

We however are not satisfied with just stopping this race or postponing it, we want to destroy it and we have plans for that also. Cannons have been hidden in the hill overlooking the beach and on a given signal they will open up and sink the majority of the paddleboats. To complete the job of destruction, a division of CRAP, which has been training in Finland for the last three months, is going to be ready to sweep across the ice on skis and throw grenades at the remaining boats. They also plan to abduct Billy Armstrong [president of the IU Foundation] and offer him as a sacrifice so that the weather of last year can be avoided and our plans for the race will not be co-opted by some of Bloomington's fine (?) temperatures.

Another front of attack shall be the golf course. Although our plans are not as complex as in other areas, we feel that we have a great chance for success at this particular battle. Our major plan is to spray the area with skin contact nerve poison and wait to see what happens when the golfers touched the grass. (Warning: wear shoes because being barefooted may be hazardous to your health.)

The high point of the war shall take place on Saturday, the day of the bike race. The rubber-seeking missiles shall be placed on top of the library and are to be used to demolish the bikes. The complete area will be sprayed with a concentrated mixture of Nitrogen Tri-Iodide which, when dried up and walked upon, will cause great explosions.

If by some act of Curt Simic [IU Foundation executive] the race progresses beyond this point, we will be ready. An added attraction this year is our tunnel from the psychology building to the middle of the field. This will be completed on or before race day and we plan to release many of the animals used in research by the Psychology department. These animals will be allowed to roam the field and the stands so watch out everyone. (Note: CRUD has been particularly interested in animals used in research dealing with methedrine and as everyone knows, SPEED KILLS!) Along with all of this action, victory pond will be well stocked with hungry piranha. We of CRUD truly apologize to our ecology friends, since we recognize the fact that the fish deserve better care and food than what they will actually receive but, unfortunately, it is the only thing we can do.

So all you people who are interested, just leave a note on your door and your friendly local CRUD agent will pay you a visit. (Note: Any contributions to CRUD will go to a fund to help pay Billy Armstrong's hospital costs in case he happens to break under the pressure.)

NOTE: We of the SPECTATOR staff hope our warning will be heeded.

From *The Spectator* X (April 15, 1970), 7.

Facing, 11. Cover, *The Spectator* IX, January 7, 1970. Art by R. T. Reece. The topics listed in the lower left-hand corner are of local interest: a strike by workers in the Bloomington plant of General Electric; trouble at Pendleton, one of the state's prisons. "Woodstock West" refers to a December 1969 concert at the Altamont Speedway in Northern California. The event was poorly managed, the sound system was bad, and some of the audience of three hundred thousand people pressed toward the stage to try to hear the music. Members of the Hells Angels motorcycle club, hired as security, began roughing up the spectators, one of whom, perhaps brandishing a gun, was stabbed to death. The Spectator included in this issue a story by Todd Gitlin, an astute and sympathetic historian of the counterculture of the 1960s. "The End of the Age of Aquarius" is Gitlin's title, and his conclusion: "That fatal component of the hippie mystique, the completion of American individualism, could too easily swamp the redeeming, negating component, the idea of solidarity.... The question is whether the youth culture will leave anything behind but a market" (9).

Voice

BY JIM CARR

SOME OF THE quote-unquote freaks around here give me a pain in the ass. I mean, they think they are the only ones who know Dylan or Tolkien or Salinger or even Marx. Hell, like I'll bet that half of the God-damn quote-unquote Communists around here don't know the difference between Karl and Groucho.

It was different a few years ago. People were really into some good things, not on ego trips. Then it wasn't cool just to have long hair and say "peace," it meant something. You know like when the [Dunn] meadow was full of people just digging the sun and each other and maybe a little stash, with dogs running and Frizzbees flying. There was—well, I don't mean to act Wordsworthian or anything—but there was a real presence, good vibrations.

Hell, they couldn't understand that now. They're too busy being quote-unquote right-on. They think they can flip through Counter-Culture, get a couple of names to quote and be heavy. Well, I'm glad that I'm outta all that jive.

From *Quarry* 2 (1973), 61.

The 60s in the 80s—Almost

BY DAVE BENDER

THE 1980S?
They're the 1960s all over again—but without the commitment.

Even protesting is back in vogue—almost. Shantytown lasted almost a year in Dunn Meadow, and a band of unruly dissenters kept [Supreme Court Chief Justice] Bill Rehnquist's dedication of the Law Library from being a total yawn.[7]

Monroe County voters kicked porn-busting Prosecutor Ron Waicukauski out of office last fall. Two feminist bookstores opened near Kirkwood. And we've even got a new "Classic Rock" radio station.

But is this "Retro-style" just a passing fancy? Are there any real hippies anymore, or is everyone just along for the ride?

Terry Anker, for example, ran unopposed for the IUSA presidency last fall. Perhaps there just wasn't anyone who could come up with a spare $3,000 to run against him. But it seems equally as likely that just nobody cared.

There weren't any riots when the sheriff's department destroyed a giant marijuana crop near Martinsville. Nobody's boycotting job interviews with Dow Chemical, or setting fire to the ROTC offices in Rawles Hall. And almost everyone on campus seems to be taking baths and wearing deodarant on a fairly regular basis.

It seems as if all this nouveau boheme has all been a matter of fashion. Not that it hasn't been fun, though.

We're wearing paisleys and leather, tie-dyes and Rasta [Rastafari] caps, ripped jeans and peasant dresses.

We ride our one-speeds to Ballantine. We drink lot of Gallo and our older brothers and sisters mail us sinsernilla [a variety of marijuana] and mushrooms.

Gone are the days when everybody came from Carmel or the Region, lived at Dunn Hill or McNutt; was a finance major.

Nowadays, we're all from California, Massachusetts, or Northbrook; live in Collins or on Second Street; study Comparative Lit or Education.

Not only that, but we find time to slop coffee at the Daily Grind, take a guitar class, play hacky-sack in Dunn Meadow, and deejay at WIUS.

It's just that we're not reading Marx or Malcolm X.

From *Arbutus*, 1987, 146.

PART SIX
·Departures·

12. "Sea of Life," by Don Herold, *Arbutus*, 1911, 36. The Monon railroad (1897–1967) provided service from Bloomington to Chicago and Louisville, and points in between.

On Entering the Campus

A Road that gently upwards leads
To where the Halls of Learning stand;
A languid brook that murmurs on;
A sunlit stretch of meadow-land.

Some knolls and hollows decked in green
Where once a mighty forest stood;
Alas, their days are numbered now—
Those monarchs of an ancient wood.

And ours? Are they not numbered, too?
Four busy years have onward rolled:
Farewell, oh trees! We may not meet
Again. Our tale is also told.

From *Arbutus*, 1915, 18.

There's Another Side of College with a Different Education

BY ROBERT SMITH

TURN THE MUSIC down; we're almost there. Okay, there's a grade school up on the hill; go past it and on the right there's a dirt road. That's it; now take it easy. It's gonna be bumpy. Where to now? Just follow the dirt path. "I can hardly see the path; ya know it's five o'clock in the morning?" There's a little cove behind that set of trees. Park the car so it'll be out of the way.

I like the morning, but only after I've stayed up all night drinking. I never could manage to drag myself out of bed early. When I was younger my family hated to wake me up in the morning. I think my family just accepted the fact that I had retained my mother's only fault—sleeping 'til noon. I knew that's what always pissed off my father. He respected the morning, like all fathers do, especially at sunrise. I respect it as long as I have a buzz going and I've been up to see the sunrise.

"Do ya think the water will be cold? I want to know if we're going to go in naked? I'd like that ya know? I've never been swimming naked with you before." Well don't sweat it; we'll swim naked, but the quarry is always cool this time of the morning. Of course after a few more beers it won't matter; the water will seem warm. Here, take my hand. The path is rocky and all you're wearing are tongs. "Josh, did you ever go swimming naked in the quarry before when it was still dark outside?" Once, I think. I thought it would be neat to bring you here. You know, two lovers watching the sunrise while their bodies are submerged in cool water. Kinda like being born again. "Quiet Josh. Listen to those birds singing. Must be getting closer to daylight. I never dreamed we would be out on a path together carrying a twelve pack of Budweiser before the sun comes up." I told you I'm in love with you Sarah; only people in love do things like this.

One more hill, blue eyes, and we'll be above the quarry. It's real peaceful out here. Man cuts the rock and makes stone then disappears and nature lives with what's left. "Look at that; it's so large. You didn't tell me it was like this." I guess some things ya can't describe with words. "This view from up on top is fantastic. It must be fifty feet down from here?" Ya know this is where they filmed the movie at. "What movie?" What movie? Christ Sarah, the only movie they ever made in Bloomington, 'Breaking Away.' "Oh yeah, sometimes you must think I'm really a space cadet or that growing up on a farm in Indiana is the sheltered life?"

Ya know Sarah the water looks so glassy this early in the morning. The wind is still and there aren't any ripples. Weird feeling isn't it. Kinda like we're going to have a born again Christian baptism. "What's wrong with going to a born again baptism?" Nothing; but do ya think they would approve of what we're doing out here? "Doubtful; heck my parents wouldn't approve of this."

Parents always expect their children to be perfect and proper. Yeah, ya gotta be proper; my father beat that into my head. Of course I used to behave properly 'til I came to IU. It must be that the temptation for sin is just overwhelming around Bloomington. Ya know after the first time I got high I never really felt temptation. I guess I don't believe in temptation and sin anymore. Bloomington does that to you.

"Okay Josh, sin a little and grab me a beer out of the cooler. This looks like a good rock to lay on." Nothing like a cold Budweiser to get things going. "Why do you always drink Budweiser?" Didn't you know? Well it's because my grandfather's father always drank Budweiser. The way I heard the story was that it was the first beer that he had had in America after emigrating to Chicago from Norway. Of course growing up in Chicago had a lot of influence on me. When I was eleven and my brother Michael was pretty much a hood, he got me plastered under the railroad overpass where we used to hang out. It was Budweiser then and has been "Bud" ever since. Rumor has it that all my brothers drink it. I don't know.

"I feel great, being out here with you. Must be something about the cool limestone and naked flesh that does it to me?" Well the Aztec Indians in Mexico used to lay out on the pyramids they built. They lasted a long time as far as civilizations go. Must have done them some good. Of course they smoked pot too. I always thought it was funny that so many civilizations in the past used drugs for pleasure; yet, it's against the law now. Progress at its best. "That smells good, what kind is it?" Sinsemilla [a variety of marijuana]. A friend of mine from Colorado grew it and sent it to me to try it out. He's into the growing scene; ya know fertilizer and all. It's nice to have friends like Paul who are always sending ya stuff to try out.

Have you ever noticed the different kinds of friends ya have? I mean there are close friends, important friends, ass-hole friends, and acquaintances. "When I first came to IU it scared me near to death to think I'd have to make new friends all over again. Coming from such a small hick town, where everyone knows everyone else's business, to massive population was freaky.

"I really hated the dorm. Have you ever tried to live with a bunch of erratic bitches?" No, not recently. "I didn't even think about becoming a sorority girl. I just couldn't imagine being a little preppie thing drooling over those obnoxious frat boys."

I never liked the idea behind Greeks either. If I needed brothers and sisters to hang out with I would have just stayed home. Being independent is where it's at anyway. Besides, I've always thought their little games of initiation were strange. Why anyone would let themselves be abused just to be part of the gang is beyond me. "They don't allow hazing anymore do they?" The hell they don't. I've had a few friends who were in fraternities. This one in particular would strip the pledges clothes off, blindfold them, make them get on their knees and chase them under chairs, beds and coffee tables while hitting them on the ass with whips. Then they'd made them eat sour milk and rotten eggs. Finally they would tie the pledges down to the kitchen table and put chemicals on their nuts that would burn the hell out of you. All in the name of brotherhood.

"I can't believe they do that."

Of course sociologists have ranked the Greek system right behind the KKK in discrimination. I know the whole Greek system here isn't like these people, but it is still wrong.

"Josh, take my hand and lead me down to the water, babe. It's nice and cool. I can't believe how glassy the water is. Kinda like your eyes." My eyes were inherited. Ya know, I pressed the right button inside my mother's womb. That's real technology—being born.

"Hold me close to you, next to your warm body. You always turn me on. When l first met you, l didn't know what to think. I was overtaken by lust. Although it was strange, l never thought someone could be as different from the rest; yet, so nice and honest. Now I'm in love with you and I still don't know what to think." Do you swim well? "Yeah I swim well; I mean if first in the region in freestyle means anything to you. I was on the swim team in high school. Hated it, but it always helped keep my body looking slender, and you like me slender don't you? How about you Josh, do you swim good?" Not really. My brother Michael taught me. He just threw me in the water one day; ya know the ole do it or die situation. So I know the essential stroke—heads up freestyle. "Come on, I'll race you. Winner gets a backrub."

It feels good to be touched like this Sarah. "You only won 'cause I'm so drunk. I always lose to you anyway, except the once or so times I've won in backgammon. Someday I'll get my reward, like a new car or a glass house." What are you talking about; you've gotten your reward. You have me, and I'm a helluva reward.

"Josh, are you sleeping?" Not really, just resting a little. Ya know it's nice to have you around. After four years of academia it makes me feel good to know I gained more than just an education. I found you; someone with whom I can share my world of feelings. I often wondered if I would ever fall in love. It's like a big void until you find that right person. "For me it's been like going through tunnels at different levels. First it was getting wasted all the time, then I went through the game of studies. I thought grades were everything. Thank God that didn't last. Then I found you in the tunnel of love; now everything fits together. I have the right amount of what I need. Although I still haven't met anyone whose day life didn't take backseat to their night life. Of course I don't spend much time in the library. I remember when we first met, and then the first time when we made love. I couldn't concentrate on anything for a week. It was always Josh, and you made me feel like I'd never been in love before."

I started thinking school would always be first, then I was introduced to vices such as pot and beer. Now it's love, and school falls further behind. I never wanted anything more out of college than experience anyway. 1 can't imagine any day without you now, even though we are still independent.

"Even though I love you Josh, you're still a bastard in the morning. I've never met anyone who hates to wake up more than you. I hope you grow out of it sometime. You remind me of a spoiled infant in the morning."

It has to be my family; they did it to me. Just like they imposed their beliefs of sin and righteousness. Sometimes I can't believe how parents raise their kids. Like the time my father threatened to punish me because I didn't want to believe in God anymore. Yelling and screaming at someone one minute and the next moment being in church asking God for control must have been his gig. I've often wondered how many "Our Fathers" he's had to say. Did he ever really confess to the priest the real man he was, or did he lie? He wasn't exactly a man of patience. My mother was the saint, and my father was the one you hid from. I grew up afraid of him, hating him, and now I want to love him but I don't know how.

"Maybe he doesn't know how Josh. He grew up in a time when they showed strength not love. Many of our parents thought being close was wrong. A child should be disciplined. 1 didn't receive any praise from dad till I was first in the 100 yd. free-style. That was in my junior year of high school. That's a long time for a daughter to wait before she knows her daddy loves her. He understands me now, and we talk now. When he decided to let me go to IU, he said in that demanding tone fathers have, 'Sarah, don't let me down; don't get pregnant and for god's sake don't ever smoke pot or I'll forget you're my daughter.' Strong words at the time. It scared the hell out of me, but now I'm older, he needs me, and I kinda understand him.

"If dad knew I lived with you he'd crap. But mom would settle the differences. Mom has always been able to control him. I get nervous when I talk with them on the phone sometimes. Like everytime we buy an ounce of pot. Ya know, PARANOID." I know the man paranoid well. He lives in my closet; hangs out there. I've never even gotten a speeding ticket and I'm paranoid. It helps sometimes. I don't do stupid things like driving the car totally wasted, but other times it's a real hangup.

Have you lit that joint yet? Thanks. "Why do you always smoke so much?" I guess it's an escape from the problems and the pressures and I need to relax. I see people better too. The parties are good to really see people at. Sometimes I like to sit in the corner and watch the people go by. The way the guys look at the girls and what they say. Ya know you can always tell a person by the way they dress? It's true. At any party I can tell you anything you want to know about a person. Except on Halloween; that's the best time. My first Halloween was the wildest. I had been invited to a party by this Jamaican friend of mine who lived off campus. I dressed up as a gay cowboy. "Come on Josh; you a gay cowboy?" Seriously now, it was great. I wore make-up, long underwear and cowboy boots. They had a huge tub of HARRY BUFFALO [Hairy Buffalo: a fruit punch with equal parts of rum, gin, vodka, tequila, and whiskey] that was very sweet tasting. My Jamaican friend dressed as a white clown. Being black, he only had to powder his face. I got plastered and could hardly walk. I hardly remember going home, but I hitched a ride along Tenth Street to Teter quad. I remember getting into the car, but that's it. My roommate, Steve, told me he found me passed out in front of our door with the keys dangling from the lock. Our suitemates helped Steve put me in bed, and I evidently told them I loved them so a rumor started that I was gay. I never did drink a Harry Buffalo again.

"People believe what they want Josh. There are real people and fake ones. I always hated the fake girls on my floor. They would play up to you; be your friend one day, then ignore you the next. The real straight ones always made me feel like I was inferior, but now I see them as they really are—fools. Fools lost in a dream. When I think back through the years in Bloomington, I've realized you are lucky if you come out of here with one close friend. Ya know someone you'll stay close to forever. Peggy is like that. To be able to trust someone with all your deepest feelings is sacred. It can't be broken. That's how I feel and I have only two people I trust—you and Peg."

Yeah. I need you too Sarah. Ya know, a lot of times Bloomington seems so unreal. I guess for our past 16+ years of schooling we've been sheltered. We don't have to worry about society's pressures. We're not there yet. We can do drugs—any drugs—we can drink beer; yet, we still always get by. Hey, we're not doing so bad. We can have pressures from classes or work and usually both. But we just smoke a joint or grab a few happy hour beers at Nick's and the pressures seem to fade away.

Bloomington doesn't give us real life. It's scary. What in the hell will it be like out there?

We don't know where we're going or if we'll make it. Why do you think I've been at IU two years past the "four year college education" quota. I keep looking for the answers to my future that just aren't here.

Anyway, grab the towel Sarah; it's getting time to go. I have a nine thirty this morning and I want to eat some breakfast. "Josh, I love you. Thanks for bringing me to this place."

We won't be here much longer but at least we have each other—for a while.

From *Arbutus*, 1983, 20–25.

The Bird

BY JOHN SCHUSTER

"BUT WE ARE all students, *ja*?" the woman said, lifting the last syllable of her sentence in a way that precluded the possibility of any reply to the contrary. Lucas blinked protectively for reprieve against her aggressive stare. One of the converted, thought Lucas.

"Yes, perhaps, but we are not all Indiana University International Students arriving at the Indianapolis Airport for the first time," said Lucas. The tall and bony German woman before him had extracted every scrap of information about the Dharana [Yoga] Foundation from Lucas that he knew offhand and eyed him reprovingly when his knowledge of minutiae and details finally gave out. Then—uninvited—she reached for a brochure intended to guide international students through the complicated orientation process of Indiana University. She certified her need for it even after Lucas explained explicitly how the pamphlet was intended for students and was of no use to a devotee on her way to meet the renowned Swami Yonyananda [apparently a fictitious name]. The German begrudgingly acknowledged Lucas's suggestion, but continued to scan the pamphlet. Then, triumphant, the woman proclaimed: "See? This tells me how to get to Indiana University in Bloomington. Which is ninety-five kilometers from here. South, I think. That is where I am going to see His Holiness!"

"Well, actually, it only tells you how to get Bloomington from the Indianapolis Airport which you already seem to know how to do. The brochure sort of implies that you realize that IU is in Bloomington. It was written for people who are going straight to IU's campus. If you are staying away from the campus you'll have to take public transportation to get there. Or a taxi. Or walk." Lucas put on his passive, stupid-looking expression he reserved for difficult foreigners and tedious professors.

"'Public transportation'? What is this?" The last syllable sprang demandingly upwards again—insisting on a simple and forthright reply even though the answer might be complex and ambiguous. It seemed that Lucas had better get this right.

"It means the bus, the city bus," said Lucas with confidence that the concept couldn't be simplified any more without resorting to a visual aid.

"*Ja*, the bus!" Temporarily satisfied, the German woman's last syllable dropped contentedly. Suddenly clutching the worn seeds strung around her neck with one hand, the woman pointed with the other at a badly printed advertisement and schedule behind scratched plexiglass and declared: "And this is the bus that will take me from here. It leaves at *forty-minutes-past-eight-o-clock*!"

Lucas gave up on getting the brochure back. It mattered little—it was only symbolic and had 500 more he was supposed to fold eventually. But in a last ditch effort to promote clarity, he said, "No, this is the *shuttle* that can take you to Bloomington. The *bus* will take you around once you *get* to Bloomington."

The German woman smiled the beneficent smile of a teacher with a dedicated if somewhat dull student. Lucas attempted a lazy sheepish smile to show the woman that he meant well and it must be some pollution in his karmic reservoir that he was not of more help in her quest to see Swami Yonyananda. He was immediately disgusted with himself for fawning and somehow felt like he had lost points in the dumb game-that-was-not-a-game. The woman clinched her victory by lighting an even more patronizing glow and turning abruptly away from him. She swished her saffron linen sun dress and strode towards the group of passively smiling middle-aged European divorcees seated near the vending machines on the far side of the ground transportation center.

Just then, one of the group of birds that had been flitting about the concourse for the last several days dive-bombed the flaxen strands that hung from the head of the German woman. The half-dozen birds—five? eight?—must have begun to build nests and were in need of raw materials.

The woman shrieked suddenly and waved her hand in the air as though warding off mosquitoes. The bird flew back from the conquest with two or three golden strands trailing from its skinny talons.

They'd been there for the last several days now. The birds were brown and nondescript. They were not distinguished birds like a cardinal or a swallow. They were the kind of birds you see perched on power lines. The kind of birds your mother is disappointed by when they come to her bird feeder. The kind of birds you see dominating the sky in enormous flocks, occasionally forming conduits of migration that stretch from one horizon to another. They were nameless, sexless birds: just birds, just small brown birds with little tufts of white on their breasts just beneath their beaks. They were probably English starlings, thought Lucas. *How ironic*—he thought—*a species so distinguished as to exist in North America because they were mentioned in Shakespeare—now has have come to typify the generic brand of birds.*[1] Unlikely as it was that the birds got into the ground transportation center the same way everyone else did—through a set of dual automatic doors—Lucas could determine no other means of entry. Unclothed by drop-ceiling sound panels, the ventilation system was exposed for easy inspection from the floor. From Lucas's vantage point leaning back in his office chair, no holes, cracks, or uncoupled ducts were visible. And the windows were intact. It could only have been through the doors—the kind with a vestibule in between designed to keep the outer and inner environments segregated—that the birds found passage. Lucas's eyes followed the German woman to her seat then closed in weariness.

Lucas ran a hand through his mop of sandy blond hair, took off his glasses, and massaged his eyes with his thumb and forefinger. His shift was almost over, thank god. His girlfriend had warned him that getting paid to greet exhausted foreigners in an airport could be more work than it might seem. He hadn't been able to imagine. Ah well. He turned back to Jomo—the nervous Kenyan education student leaning against the side of the booth whose ongoing life saga was interrupted by the Aryan woman.

As Lucas was about to address Jomo, a small swarthy man approached with a young woman—almost supermodel-esque in proportion—following him. "Hello!" the man said with enthusiasm, "I saw your sign." He pointed to the handmade sign adorning to the top of the booth that welcomed IU International Students with bold, multi-colored lettering and exclamation points. The man continued with an enthusiasm that was now obviously feigned, "I think we are the people you are looking for."

"Well!" said Lucas, lighting a smile. "Welcome to the United States! Are you going to Bloomington?" The man stopped at the front of the booth and adjusted the collar on his khaki sport coat. He took a deep breath, straightened the wrinkles in his outfit as though it was a tunic, and smiled patronizingly at Lucas.

"Am I going to Bloomington, you ask," he said with a small smile. "Yes, I am going to Bloomington. Let me tell you where I have been. Thirty-eight hours ago I left Veroia in a taxi. I arrived in Thessaloniki. From Thessaloniki we—my daughter and I—took the ferry to Athens. From Athens we took a small plane to Rome. From Rome we took a large jet across the Atlantic Ocean to New York City. From New York City we flew to Detroit, Michigan. From Detroit we took a very small plane here to Indianapolis. Now we are here in Indianapolis and all my daughter and I want to do is get a motel room." At the mention of his daughter, the man motioned for the statuesque young woman to step forward. He put an arm around her. He continued, "We have an early appointment with the dean of your Classics department and—yes—we would like to go to Bloomington to get some rest. Do you know how we might do that?"

Before saying anything, Lucas began nodding his head. Just as he was about speak, a white and yellow smudge suddenly appeared on the man's shoulder. Lucas didn't say anything. No one had noticed, not even the man's daughter. Lucas couldn't help but smile just a bit and as he did the Greek girl shifted some dark curls from Lucas and smiled back. Her father noticed she was smiling and smiled all around. Even at Jomo. Jomo smiled too. Lucas cleared his throat.

"I think you've come to the right place," said Lucas casually as he straightened his back. He looked the man in the eye and smiled and then did the same to the girl.

"Ah great," said the man with a deliberately rolled R. "I would like one round trip and one one-way trip to Bloomington please."

"Ok great," said Lucas, "You'll buy your tickets from the bus driver. He should be back any minute now. I can come find you if you like to let you know when he's back."

The Greek man flexed the corner of his mouth wryly at Lucas as though inviting to please share in the absurdity of the situation. Lucas demurred by looking again at the man's daughter. She looked back. The Greek man said brusquely, "Yes, all right. Fine. We'll be sitting over there." He twisted his midsection and pointed across the room as his stiff khaki sport coat bunched around his shoulders. Lucas nodded amiably at the Greeks and began to fold brochures. As the Greek man left with his daughter in tow, Lucas turned his attention back to Jomo, the Kenyan. "So there are many bicycles available," said Lucas half-heartedly, picking up where he had left off. He sensed that he might be keeping the man company until the next shuttle departed: forty-minutes-past-eight-o-clock. Lucas had reviewed the process of acquiring a bicycle in Bloomington three times now after running short of other conversation ideas an hour ago. But he persisted because Jomo seemed so contented to be hearing anything at all. Lucas was beginning to feel like a salesman. He should get a commission. He went on, "With your price range, you could go to a store called K-Mart to get a new bike. But I'd suggest getting a used bike. You'll get a much better deal. Also, someone told me that the police occasionally auction off stolen bicycles that they impounded." Lucas sat back from the man....

"Well, I'm just the hairy-legged ol' boy who kin get you to Bloomington!" It was Dean—the shuttle driver—confirming an inquiry about his occupation and trundling purposefully towards the booth Lucas shared with the Sycamore Shuttle Service. A deferent young Indian woman followed him to the booth as she fished around in a new nylon backpack. Lucas watched her eyes widen through oversized rimless glasses as she observed Dean limp around the booth and set about depositing his bulk into the coffee-stained ergonomic office chair next to Lucas's. Lucas turned to watch the familiar ritual. "Welcome back, Dean," he said as he rolled the chair back a little. "Have a seat."

"Don't mind if do, don't mind if do," said Dean in his best W.C. Fields impression. Dean's face acquired a look of concentration and he grunted a bit as he reached back to grasp the vinyl armrests to balance himself and prevent the chair from rolling away. Then the bottom crease of his inward-sloping buttocks found purchase at the edge of the chair. His expression changed minutely acknowledging the attainment. His brow then furrowed, he breathed out forcefully, twisted his midsection to wedge it between the armrests, then gave the task over to gravity, leaned back, and in a controlled fall settled back into the chair. His thighs tensed as he gripped the floor with the rubber soles of his shoes to keep from rolling. He relaxed momentarily, squirmed and shook a bit to settle everything properly on the foundation of his prodigious bus driver's ass, he adjusted his glasses on the bridge of his nose, and he rubbed his bad knee some. He turned to Lucas and said, "Been holding down the fort while I was gone, buddy?" Lucas nodded agreeably and Dean redirected his attention to the Indian girl.

"Now what can I do you for, young lady?" he said with a wink. The girl quickly regained her composed, semi-automatic smile and resumed fishing in her backpack. I don't need that, she seemed to think, nor that. What else don't I need? Not that either. Not ready to look up, she said, "I would like to go to Bloomington on the shuttle, please." Her voice retained some of the clipped rhythms of her native Indian English, but through the medium of satellite TV, it had been infected with the causal insouciance of American youth. Dean lifted his chin in a gesture of approval, set his clipboard on the counter, began to unclip things, and readied himself to accommodate. "Wunwayerrountrip, young lady?"

"Pardon me? I want one ticket only," the girl said. Confused and unaccustomed to dealings with presumptuously familiar and presumptuously large white men, the girl had no idea what to make of the bus driver, who looked at her from beneath bushy eyebrows. She seemed to shrink as she slipped back into the deferent, yielding deportment of her upbringing. She seemed torn between crawling into her backpack or moving slightly closer to Dean in order to hear him better. Her eyes turned to the less threatening figure of Lucas but despite wanting to help Lucas hesitated.

Dean eyed Lucas carefully. Lucas opened his mouth to talk but Dean cut him off before he could say anything. "Now Lucas," he said, "Goshdamit we've been through this. These are *my* customers right now. When they're talking to you about IU they are your people but when they're buying tickets from me, they're my people and I'll take care of them."

Lucas closed his mouth. Dean could be much louder as he proved the last time Lucas tried to "meddle." In that case it was a Peruvian girl who spoke no English. Lucas spoke Spanish to her in an attempt to facilitate communication between Dean and his customer. Dean did not appreciate the help, cut Lucas off, and proceeded to gradually raise his voice at the girl until—close to tears—she handed over enough money for a round trip ticket when she needed only a one-way. Fearing another outburst, Lucas desisted from confronting Dean and took the opportunity to ogle at the Greek girl. She flicked her glance to Lucas, then to one of the birds that was traversing the upper reaches of the ground transportation center, then was reabsorbed into the romance novel she was reading.

Dean took a moment to grin licentiously at what Lucas had distracted himself with. He then turned back to the Indian girl, breathed deep and drawing on his limited store of patience for people who didn't slur the English language the way he did, he settled into the ordeal. Unlike Indian hospitality, American Southern hospitality is proud and unforgiving. But he re-enunciated his question a hair slower: "Wun-way'r-roun-trip?"

The girl still looked confused and looked imploringly at Lucas, but Lucas turned his chair towards the wall of glass to his left and cracked his knuckles. The late summer weather outside was bright and blotchy, car exhaust and jetliner contrails mixing with a few clouds and smoke from distant smokestacks. Just beyond the glass, huge busses lumbered in and out of small parking spaces like well-herded cattle. Just in front of a plate glass window, a hired policeman was dozing at one end of a rack of chairs—a linked set with armrests in between to deter people from lying down on them and monopolizing the sitting space. Across from him a muted television played syndicated sitcoms. At the other end of the bench, a gaily-dressed man from Cameroon wearing a skullcap quietly plunked an *m'bira* —a small thumb piano—and occasionally eyed Jomo—an East African—suspiciously. He stopped suddenly and looked to his left with raised eyebrows, clearly distracted by something. Lucas followed his gaze and saw one of the birds flying—almost aiming—right at the plate glass wall. It smacked into it with a muffled but audible thump.

The bird slammed into the glass wall several times before alighting on a bank of arrival/departure [video] terminals. Lucas did not recognize the bird but then again they all looked alike.

The bird hopped about for a bit as though dazed, but eventually it flitted down from the monitors and pecked at the crumbs of potato chips and packaged pastries that littered the general seating area. Perhaps it was lured indoors by promise of the meager sustenance it was now consuming. Lucas remembered a possibly apocryphal story about a distinct species of birds that had somehow evolved to survive in the enclosed environment of some large airport in Europe. Lucas thought it might have been in Belgium. Meanwhile, having pecked at several dozen bagel crumbs, bits of pretzel salt, and other such refuse, the bird lit from the floor and landed in a planter of artificial vegetation. Camouflaged by the waxy plastic leaves, the bird hopped from border to border of the fake foliage and surveyed the area with staccato head movements. It seemed to teeter back and forth on its legs then tried to fly off. It made it about four feet before falling to the floor. After fluttering about on the ground, it flitted back up to the planter. The man from Cameroon, the Greek girl, and several people were observing the bird in rapture.

Inspired by the opportunity for distraction and petty heroism, Lucas made fast plans to rescue the trapped bird. He quickly but quietly emptied his satchel, crept up to the planter, and smothered the bird with his bag. The bird struggled—thumping its frail wings against the synthetic material—and chirped excitedly in fear and protest. Lucas threw an arm over the bag to secure the bag and the bird within. As his muscles relaxed, he could feel the bird struggling and felt the beat of its small heart beating quickly. How frail it seemed, how lightweight. The Greek girl had looked up from her orientation pamphlet to stare dumbly at Lucas. Lucas gripped the outside of the bag to still the bird. How easy it would be to crush that bird. It would be instantaneous. Lucas looked at the Greek girl and ran to the doors.

Lucas moved as quickly through the automatic doors as he could and immediately threw open the satchel to release the bird. As the bird was released from the bag, it seemed to hover in midair like a hummingbird. Lucas watched the bird float. For a moment he saw the whole of the ground transportation reflected in its convex eye. Lucas reached out suddenly for the bird but came back with only a tail feather. He watched the bird fly clumsily to clear skies as a few people back in the terminal applauded briefly and half-ironically. He put the feather in his back pocket as he walked back in. The man from Cameroon was playing a bright, lilting melody on his thumb piano, Dean was squinting in exasperation at his next customer, and the Greek girl had found a fashion magazine to look at.[2]

From *Labyrinth*, 2000, 4–10.

APPENDIX
Student Publications at Indiana University Bloomington

FEW SOURCES EXIST that detail the history of student publications on Indiana University's campus in Bloomington. One source, Ivy L. Chamness's chapter on "University Publications" (712–17) in the second volume (1952) of the *History of Indiana University*, by Burton D. Myers, provides a well-informed and important introduction to the character and history of these magazines (689–717). Ms. Chamness (1881–1975), who received an AB in journalism from IU in 1906, was assistant and then principal editor of university publications from 1914 until her retirement in 1952. She also served as editor of the *IU Alumni Quarterly* until 1938. In a response to an inquiry about Ms. Chamness's work, James Capshew, University Historian, writes that she made that publication into a forum for writing on the history of the university so that it became "the journal of record for the history of IU." Ms. Chamness understood that all the catalogs, bulletins, and other official documents whose editing she supervised were "grist for the mill of the historian" (712), and in her stewardship and careful account of these documents in her chapter she became, to quote Professor Capshew again, "the de facto gatekeeper of the official history of IU."

In her chapter on official university publications, Ms. Chamness admits that they "provide no chuckles. For a picture of the light side of University life we go to student publications" (712). Earlier in her chapter, she mentions ideas for two literary publications that were not proposed by students, one of which did not make it into print. She quotes a motion, never acted upon, to the Board of Trustees in 1839 "to procure and establish a literary paper ... under the direction of the board" (691). And she describes *The Equator*, a weekly paper published in the 1840s, which was, in its own words, "devoted to the interests of Science and Literature in the West" (692). Principally, however, the journal was a vehicle for President Andrew Wiley to distribute his own writing and news about the university.

"Probably the first student publication," Ms. Chamness writes, "was *The Athenian*" (712), published in 1845. She does not mention *The Dagger* (1875-79?) or its successor *The Scourge* (1880)—two annuals often given to harsh criticism of faculty and mean-spirited gossip about students. In a letter included in the file of the latter in the University Archives, she advises a librarian, perhaps with tongue in cheek, to keep it "under lock and key, inasmuch as some well-known persons are mentioned in a very unkind manner."

Ms. Chamness did have at hand some magazines that are no longer listed in the catalog of the university library—for example, *The Bumble Bee* (1899), *The Hoosier "Lit"* (1901), and *The Crimson Quill* (about 1927). I have included these titles in the list that follows, even though I have not seen any of their issues. I cite the current location of all the other student publications I have read.

In the first volume of his *History of Indiana University 1820-1902* (1940), James Albert Woodburn also names and comments on a half dozen student magazines published on campus around the turn of nineteenth century (444-48).

Some information about the character and history of a student magazine is often included in its entry in the university library (IUCAT) catalog when the magazine is digitized and put online. These informative and very useful accounts are prepared by members of the Archives staff.

The Athenian, 1845-46. Published by the Athenian Society. "We wish to make *The Athenian* an advocate of chaste and elevated literature" (I: December 1845, 3). The membership of the Athenian Society, at least in its early years, was all male. Also in volume 1 (April 1846): "A word to our lady readers.—Will you not enliven the pages of the Athenian with your contributions?" (23) University Archives.

An Olio of Love and Song. Delivered before the Athenian Society of Indiana University, July 3, 1855, by Sidney Dyer. Published by the Athenian Society, 1855. Archives.

The Dagger, 1875–79. Annual written and published during commencement by members of the Beta Theta Pi fraternity. Final number is dated 1880, but in an "explanation" on the first page its editors claim that the paper appears "a year before its time" because "an emergency exists." The emergency was current but not new: the editors returned to their complaint about the appointment of faculty members subservient to the president's ideas. Harsh criticism of Presidents Nutt and Moss, of some faculty members, and of students. Archives.

The Scourge, 1880. Successor to *The Dagger*: annual published during commencement by members of Beta Theta Pi. Same format and style as *The Dagger*. Archives.

Arbutus, 1894. Yearbook of the Bloomington campus. Archives; Wells Library; online.

The I. U. Illustrator, 1897. Chamness, Woodburn. No copies available.

The Bumble Bee: A Literary Publication. Chamness, Woodburn. Named in *Arbutus*, 1899. No copies available.

The Hoosier "Lit.": Magazine of Indiana Stories, Sketches, and Poems. Edited by students at Indiana University. Bimonthly. Chamness, Woodburn. Named in *Arbutus*, 1901. No copies available.

As She Is, 1901. Chamness, Woodburn. No copies available.

Megaphone, 1900. A yearbook published by the junior class, entered as "first-class matter at the office of the Department of English." Chamness, Woodburn. Archives. Other junior yearbooks named by Chamness: *Hot Shots*, 1901; *The Junior*, 1905, 1906, 1911.

The Crimson, 1909. Chamness. No copies available.

The Hoosier: A Literary Magazine, 1916–20. Monthly during the school year. Publication of the Writers Club, Department of English. Wells.

The Crimson Bull, 1920–21. Monthly during the school year. Published by Sigma Chi Delta, a fraternity of professional journalists. When the magazine began to make money, its manager absconded with it (*The Bored Walk*, January 1932, 14). One issue (November 1920) in Archives.

The Vagabond, 1923–31. Advertised as bimonthly during the academic year, although sometimes combined last two numbers of the year into one issue. "Its object is two-fold: the magazine offers a medium of expression for the literary life of the campus; and it hopes to hasten a rebirth of interest in science, art, and life in Indiana" (I: 1, 33–34). Open to undergraduates, alumni, faculty. Archives; online.

The Crimson Quill. About 1927. Chamness. No copies available.

The Bored Walk, 1931–42. Monthly during the school year. "You students at Indiana University, readers of Bored Walk, are cynical, satirical, sarcastic, twinkling, spicy, slangy, and modern.... BORED WALK, this year, intends to be like you. It hopes to portray you to yourself. It aims to present an alive, interesting, ever moving record of campus life as it is at Indiana NOW" (IX:1 1939, 3). And in the following year: "BORED WALK is a humor magazine, touching lightly on the theological, moral, ethical, and philosophical side of life, with frequent suggestions concerning the improvement of the soul.... To offset the light side, we deal very slightly in a deeper side through our editorial columns. It isn't always so deep. But we do have a platform. We are strictly against most things" (XI:1 1940, 3).

The Bored Walk suspended publication in October 1942 after it published an issue that, according to a note in the journal's entry in the digital IU library catalog, contained some jokes of a sexual nature and "rude remarks" about the Catholic Church. The comptroller of the university,

Ward Biddle, judged the magazine "no longer decent enough to be distributed as the product of Indiana University students." Archives; online.

Folio: A Quarterly for Writers at Indiana University, 1936–60. "We present THE FOLIO, the fruition of an idea: That there is a definite place for a publication to encourage and develop creative writing at Indiana University and its Extension Centers; That such a publication should combine artistic format with readable modern typography; That such a publication should be self-supporting through voluntary subscriptions and advertising" (I:1 1936, 1).

Early issues were used as textbooks in elementary composition courses: "It is my hope that the whole issue will serve as a workshop" (V:3 1940, 25). Then it changed to an undergraduate literary magazine: "In the palpable quickening of creativeness on the campus, the newly formulated policy for student direction of *The Folio* can play a significant part." At this point it was no longer edited by faculty, nor would it serve primarily "as a medium for the publication of classroom work. Now . . . *The Folio* becomes a literary magazine accepting contributions from all university students and selecting its material strictly on the basis of literary merit" (VI: 3 1941, inside front cover). In the 1950s, it changed again to become a standard literary little magazine, edited by graduate students and publishing writing by well-known national and international writers. Archives.

Snafoo, 1945. Weekly. Gossip about Greek houses and dorms, jokes, complaints about bookstores and overzealous house mothers. Directed at returning veterans, but its early demise was predicted in a headline in its second and perhaps final issue: "Veterans Meet. 17 Present. 300 in School" (January 29, 1945, 1). Wells.

The Date, 1946–47. Monthly during the school year. "The 'lux' in the Indiana University trademark means 'Keep light.' The first mark of a cultivated man is the ability to 'Keep light.'" (I:1 1946, 28). Archives, online.

The Crimson Bull, 1947–56. Monthly during the school year. Published by Sigma Delta Chi. "All hail to the CRIMSON BULL, a new magazine with an old, traditional name! A big, lusty name for a big, lusty university ... a name that rings on your lips ... and deftly suggests the raciness of Dame Satire that lies so innocently between the covers." The *Bull* is back, "back to blow his derisive breath in our face, to jab us pointedly with his great horns... back with a stinging power in his great hulk... back with verve and zest so necessary for the spinning pace of today's campus!" (I: 1 1947, 3). Archives; online.

The Indiana Renegade, c.1952. Monthly. Advertised as *The Renegade* on the cover of *The Crimson Bull* (May 1952). Two issues, undated, in Archives.

Pegasus, 1962–67. Semiannual. Published by the Department of English. Wells.

The Spectator, 1966–70. Weekly during the school year. Summer edition 1969. "A weekly newspaper review, THE SPECTATOR seeks to present the best of two mediums, the newspaper and the periodical review. The emphasis in both areas will be on responsible reporting and quality writing.... THE SPECTATOR will in no way represent or advocate the beliefs of any campus organization or any specific political ideology" (February 5, 1966, 4). Wells.

The Inside Agitator, 1967–68. Weekly. Published by the Progressive Reform Party. Wells.

The Alternative, An American Spectator, 1967–77. Monthly during the school year. "We will gently offer more civilized substitutions to the panaceas averred by disturbed adolescents of the new left" (I: 1 1967, 2). Always national in its ambitions, it later moved from Bloomington to Arlington, VA, and was renamed *The American Spectator*. Archives.

The Ballantonian: A Liberal Arts Review, 1967–69. Weekly during the school year. Sponsored by the Department of English. The *Indiana Daily Student* does not give adequate in-depth coverage "to the rich academic and cultural atmosphere of Indiana University," and *The Spectator* has moved far left and "has become so politically oriented and scatological in its content that any claim to literary value is a farce.... We are a liberal arts review, and will present reviews of political issues from time to time, but in no way will we be oriented to the left or to the right through our editorials" Notable for excellent, measured reporting (by Paul Briand) on campus antiwar demonstrations. (I; 1, 1967, 1). Archives.

Son of Ballantonian: A Libidinal Arts Review, 1969. Will leave political issues "in the undoubtedly good hands of THE SPECTATOR and THE ALTERNATIVE" and will provide the "broadest possible camp" for coverage of the arts (February 20, 1969, 1). Archives.

The Black Wheel, 1970. Office of Afro-African Affairs. One issue. Mimeographed. "Organ for the dissemination of Black news, thoughts, discussions, and art through the campus." Lilly Library.

Quarry: An Undergraduate Journal of the Arts, 1972–78, 1981–98. Biannual. "*Quarry* publishes work by students from all levels of the Creative Writing Program in the Department of English. It appears with funding from the Department of English" (1972 I, 1). Staff is composed entirely of students (VI: Spring 1975, back cover). "For three years *Quarry* was comatose, or at least in a deep sleep. We revived it because we felt that there was a need for an undergraduate literary magazine." Funding now from Indiana University student activities fund (IX: 1981, 3). Wells.

Dancing Star, 1976–. Annual. Collins Living-Learning Center. "Dancing Star is a nifty little magazine published rather sporadically by a small group of students in hopes of being an open forum of sorts for the creative endeavors of the student communities of MRC-Collins" (1977). Archives.

Collins Columns, 1979–. Collins Living-Learning Center. Began as an unnamed mimeographed newsletter and calendar of events. Named in January 1981 and began to publish poetry and commentary. Weekly during the school year. Archives; Collins.

Labyrinth, 1986–. Annual. "*Labyrinth* is a literary magazine published by the Academic Unit Coordinating Committee, in hopes of becoming a forum of sorts for the creative endeavors of the student community of the Academic Units of Indiana University" (1989, inside front cover). Later: "The Undergraduate Magazine of the Indiana University Honors Division" (1997). Wells; Archives.

Calliope, 1994. Collins Living-Learning Center. Archives.

Canvas, 1996?–. "*Canvas* is a biannual publication featuring poetry, prose, visual art created by the Fine Arts Committee [of the Union Board]." Spring 2002. Archives. Issues online https://imu.indiana.edu/union-board/canvas/index.html

Cocked and Ready, 1999–2000. Biannual. Collins Living-Learning Center. "*Cocked and Ready* is the only local literary magazine where the focus of each issue is to gather the best poetry and short fiction, work hand in hand with the authors to edit their pieces, and establish a focused, well-constructed artifact documenting young, modern writing" (II:1, 2000). Included CDs of student performances. Archives.

Other publications published in Men's Residence Center/Collins; stored with Collins material in Archives:

South Hall Citadel, 1927. Mostly a yearbook: "a review of the most important events in the life of the dormitory this year." South Hall, a men's dormitory, opened in 1924. In 1940 it became part of the Men's Residence Center, which in turn became the Living-Learning Center in 1972, named for Ralph Collins in 1980.

The Hall's Echo, 1950–52. Newspaper. "Armed Forces Take Forty Men from Quad."

MRC Tower, 1967. Mimeographed. Mostly a newsletter.

Living-Learning Center Journal, 1973.

Flypaper, 1973–74.

The Bystander: A Monthly Review of Books, Poetry and Manners, Written and Published by Collins-LLC residents, 1981. Will offer "opportunities for the untrammeled expression of individual opinion" (February 1981). Ed. Nick Cullather.

The Gadfly, 1986. "Will publish commentary, news, theory, art, fiction"—for example, "Apathy at IU," "The US in Honduras."

Vague, 1995. "Collins Columns is not accepting any literary things, and the Dancing Star does not begin until the spring. *Vague* is the creative forum for the fall."

A Book of Seven Souls, n.d. All poetry.

vegan alternative, 1998–2005. Online weekly newsletter. A lot of poetry.

Potty Talk, 2000–02. Edmundson fourth floor publication. Women's health update; how departments grade; Philosophy: "What is a grade?"

A Piece of Crap, 2002. *Onion* style: "Collins Student Refuses to Harm Celery."

The Gnome Legacy, 2003 Newsletter and columns of opinion: "Cliques at Collins."

April 16 (Next Thursday), 2009.

Good Omens, n.d. Graphic narratives.

Dancing Stark Naked, n.d. Poetry and short fiction.

Collins Speaks: The Collected Writings of the Collins Writing Society, n.d.

Also: *Ralph*, a telephone directory organized by first names of Collins' residents; *The Boyz of Collins*, mock male cheesecake calendar; Collins Haggedah.

The Pipe and the Barrow, 2010–. A Collins magazine that publishes student papers written for courses conducted in the Living-Learning Center; one of several journals founded in the last twenty years or so that are given to academic papers written by undergraduates. All are sponsored by academic units or offices, and all are edited by undergraduates, with advice from members of the faculty. In its first number, *Primary Sources: Indiana University Undergraduate Journal of History* (2012–) described itself as founded by undergraduates with the purpose of bringing "undergraduates into the historical conversation" (I:1, 2012).

The Undergraduate Scholar, 2012–. Sponsored by the Hutton Honors Program, welcomes "submissions from current Indiana University students in all areas of study" (I: 2012).

The Indiana University Journal of Undergraduate Research, 2015–. Sponsored by the office of the vice provost for undergraduate education on the

Bloomington campus. Publishes papers written by students on all campuses of the university, including professional schools on the Indianapolis campus (it has published papers by students in medicine and mechanical engineering).

In their purpose of giving undergraduates and students in the professional schools a chance to practice the tactics of discovery and display that they are learning in their studies, these publications are somewhat like the programs and journals sponsored by nineteenth-century literary societies. True, sometimes the ideas and methods of the papers are peculiar to contemporary research ("RNA-seq Analysis of lncRNAs and cis NATS in the Tomato Genome": *Journal of Undergraduate Research*, 2015). But in kind if not in content, the topics of others—"The Inner Battle of the Civil War: Lew Wallace's Views on Slavery" (*Primary Sources*, spring 2012); "Bosnia and Herzegovina: A Nation Divided" (*Undergraduate Scholar*, spring 2015); and "The Sand Creek Massacre," *Journal of Undergraduate Research* (I:1, 2015)—would have been familiar to members of the nineteenth-century Athenian and Philomathean societies.

NOTES

PART ONE: THE CAMPUS AND THE TOWN

1. Editor's note. Renamed Eagleson Avenue in 2021. The section of the street that runs through campus was renamed for the late distinguished professor of music David Baker. I have retained throughout the names of buildings, streets, and other features of the campus and town as they were known at the time of the publication of the story, essay, or poem.

2. William Moenkhaus, a student and friend of Carmichael, was a gifted musician, composer, and surrealistic poet who died young. He is the subject of a eulogy by B. Winifred Merrill, head of the department and then of the School of Music, in *The Vagabond* (VII, 3, 1931), 11–12.

3. Smoke-ups: midterm warnings of inadequate grades or excessive absences.

4. Hargis Westerfield was a student and teaching assistant in the Department of English. He served in the infantry during the campaign in New Guinea during World War II, wrote a history of his unit, and has published several books of poetry.

5. Jonathan Adler was a colleague of Ms. Chapman's on *Canvas*; in O'Hara's poem the reference is to the American writer Edwin Denby. Heath Ledger (1979–2008), film actor; Sydney Pollack (1936–2008), film director.

6. Robert Laurent's sculpture, *The Birth of Venus*, is in the Fine Arts Plaza in front of the Auditorium.

PART TWO: STUDENTS

1. The chapel was part of a building on the original campus of the university. It was used for lectures by members of the faculty and visitors, assemblies, commencement, and other university events, including "Morning Prayers," conducted at 8:00 a.m. or, later, 10 a.m. Attendance was compulsory for students. The campus then was on a site bounded by First and Second and Walnut and Morton Streets; part of this site is now called Seminary Square. After the fire of 1883, the

campus was moved to its present location, and the purposes of the chapel were moved to a building that became Mitchell Hall, torn down in 1986.

2. Priapus was a god of fertility and, among other responsibilities, the protector of male genitalia. The caverns of Phigalia, a Greek city, were said to contain a figure of the Black Demeter, goddess of the harvest and thus also of fertility.

3. Movies vs. a play by George Bernard Shaw; art by a very successful if sometimes superficial painter (Parrish) vs. that by an artist of dark and disturbing compositions (Kent); fiction by a best-selling writer of exotic romance (*The Sheik*, 1921) vs. the difficult stories of Joseph Conrad: until the middle of the last century it was a commonplace among young sophisticates like Davis that popularity and commercial success were signs of a debased and superficial form of art.

4. Goldie Typical is the central character of another story by Frank Smith in *The Vagabond* (II:1 1924). Like Nell, Goldie enters the university excited by the adventure of learning. Unlike Nell, who cannot get beyond the superficial excitements of her education, Goldie drifts into a degraded idea of academic success and becomes a calculating student who chooses courses in which she can get good grades and joins clubs that make her visible on campus. In their different ways, both stories discount the ambitions and intellectual capacities of women.

5. *The Beggar's Opera*, drama by John Gay (1728); *Fantomina*, protofeminist novel by Eliza Haywood (1725); *Perfect Blue*, animation by Pafekuto Buru (1997); *Tokyo Idols*, documentary film by Kyoko Miyake about girl bands and their music; *Raw*, French horror film written and directed by Julia Ducournau (2016); *Mrs. Dalloway*, novel by Virginia Woolf (1925); "The Dead," short story in *Dubliners*, by James Joyce (1914).

PART THREE: FACULTY

1. Charles Sembower (1871–1947) was a member of the English faculty from 1892 to 1941. As an undergraduate at Indiana (BA 1892), he had played varsity baseball, and he remained intensely interested in intercollegiate athletics. Sembower Field, the predecessor to the present baseball stadium on the Bloomington campus, was named for him.

2. William Lowe Bryan (1860–1955) served as president of Indiana University from 1902 to 1937. After studying philosophy and classics at IU (BA 1884, MA 1886), he completed a doctorate (1892) at Clark in experimental psychology and returned to the university in 1893 as professor of psychology. During his presidency he frequently wrote short, often homiletic pieces for campus publications, in which he was also often written about as mentor and sage.

3. Guido Stempel, English, comparative philology; Alfred Mansfield Brooks, fine arts; Charles Campbell, head of the Department of Music; Carl Eigenmann, zoology, director of the Biological Station; William Evans Jenkins, English, University Librarian.

4. In *Indiana University Bloomington: America's Legacy Campus* (Bloomington: Indiana University Press, 2017), J. Terry Clapacs writes that several boardwalks were constructed and dismantled to meet changing patterns of foot traffic and conditions of the grounds (45–47). The walk Don Herold describes (see also the reference to the Board Walk in George Shively's novel) ran from Kirkwood Hall to the site on which Ballantine Hall now stands, whose construction required the elimination of Forest Place.

5. A Skinner box is a chamber used to study animal behavior. It was invented by B. F. Skinner, a member of the Indiana University Department of Psychology, 1945–48.

6. Like Mickey Spillane, Jack Woodford was a very popular novelist. Jimmy Durante, a comedian and singer, signed off his radio shows by bidding good night to Mrs. Calabash, a nickname for his wife.

PART FOUR: ROMANCE

1. The story is set at the biological field station, established in Kosciusko County in 1895, by Carl Eigenmann.

PART FIVE: PROTESTS

1. Cyrus Nutt (1814–75) was president of the university from 1860 until shortly before his death in 1875. His successor, Lemuel Moss (1829–1904), president of the university from 1875 to 1884, was at first judged by a writer in *The Dagger* as "as a President of rare talent" (1878, 1) But in 1880, in the same journal, he was described as man of "haughty but contemptible arrogance," capable of "wolfish chicanery and fox-like deception" (1) who, according to his critics, appointed to the faculty persons whose principal qualification was their readiness to support the president.

2. Frank Merriwell is the hero of a series of early twentieth-century sports novels.

3. At the beginning of 1942, the university inaugurated an accelerated curriculum that enabled students to graduate in two and a half years.

4. The photograph that the *Arbutus* board refused to publish in the yearbook was of a group of young women, two of them Black, meeting for lunch in the Union. The photograph was originally published in a Black newspaper in Indianapolis.

5. During World War II, the Army Specialized Training Program enrolled enlisted men in programs in foreign languages, engineering, and medicine on college and university campuses.

6. In Kurt Vonnegut's novel *Cat's Cradle*, Ice-9 is a chemical substance that turns liquids into solids.

7. The 1987 *Arbutus* contained two essays pertinent to this comment. One was about Shantytown, a collection of shacks and tents in Dunn Meadow housing students who were protesting the university's failure to divest its investment in South African securities. Thehe other was about the demonstrations when Supreme Court Justice William Rehnquist spoke in the auditorium and at the dedication of the new law library.

PART SIX: DEPARTURES

1. Starlings are the sole survivors of a late-nineteenth-century attempt to introduce into America every species of bird mentioned in Shakespeare's writing.

2. Although this story is not set on campus, or even in Bloomington, it touches on two features common in campus life: the international character of the university and the tension and difference between town (Dean) and gown (Lucas). (See also *People from Bloomington* [Penguin, 2022], a translation of short stories by the distinguished Indonesian writer Budi Darma, who studied in Bloomington and graduated with a doctorate in English in 1980.) The adventures of the bird may be taken as a metaphor for going to college. Closed in the space of the ground transportation lounge of the Indianapolis airport, the bird tries various paths of flight, bangs against the wall a few times, and then, with some capable assistance, releases itself into the open sky of the rest of its life.

ACKNOWLEDGMENTS

FIRST OF ALL, Susan Gubar, my late-life love, the sea that sustains me and the anchor that keeps me steady. Susan took me on innumerable trips to the library so that I could look at the books and journals I gathered for this project, kept reminding me that the project was a good idea, and offered very important advice about the arrangement of the collection. Without Susan, this book, and much else, could not have happened.

James Capshew, university historian and faculty member in the IU Department of the History and Philosophy of Science and Medicine, suggested this project to me, and all along the way to its completion he found material I should read and answered questions about the history of the Bloomington campus. The biographer of Herman B Wells, Jim holds an idea of a public university and a knowledge of the traditions of the Bloomington campus that are good for us to remember.

When I began reading for the project, Dina Kellams, director of the IU Archives, put together for me a list of the titles of a couple dozen student magazines published on the Bloomington campus, whose contents turned out to be the foundation of this anthology. Bradley Cook, curator of photographs in the Archives staff, prepared photographs of the illustrations in the book and continued to answer my questions even while it was being copyedited. Other members of the Archives well-informed and capable staff also suggested new titles for me to consider and were quick to answer questions about what I was finding.

Leigh Davis, of the IUB Collins Living-Learning Center, helped me find and use material from the Collins Center library during a summer when it was closed.

Jason Michelak, my research assistant and a graduate student in the Department of English, and Bre Anne Briskey, a graduate student in the Department of the History and Philosophy of Science and Medicine and a research assistant for James Capshew, worked to convert the texts of the prose and poetry in this book into Word files. Jason also helped me with proofreading the texts.

Julie Gray's intelligence and editorial experience were invaluable in bringing the book to its final form. Gary Dunham, director of the Indiana University Press, and Michelle Mastro, an editor at the press, asked for cuts in the bulk of matter I submitted. The excisions, painful as they were to execute, made clear some continuities between the texts and, I've got to say, made the whole book more buoyant and easier to read.

I also thank Kelly Kish, director of the Office of the Bicentennial, for enrolling the book in the bicentennial project and for helping toward its publication.

Finally, I thank the writers and artists who granted permission for the publication of their work in this collection. I also pay tribute to the founders and editors of the student journals who gave their contemporaries space and occasions in which to explore what it meant, in their moment, to be a university student on the Bloomington campus of Indiana University.

DONALD J. GRAY came to the Bloomington campus as an instructor in English in 1956, retired as Culbertson professor of English in 1997, and put together the anthology during the bicentennial year of the university, with help from James Capshew, the university historian, and the staff of the university archives.

www.ingramcontent.com/pod-product-compliance
Lightning Source LLC
Chambersburg PA
CBHW020837020526
44114CB00040B/1228